everyday Low fat

everyday Low fat

MURDOCH
BOOKS

contents

The Low-down on Low-fat

Eating low-fat isn't the same as being on a diet, but rather a change in eating habits that can stay with you for life, altering your tastes for good. Can't imagine a world without mayonnaise and cream? We'll show you how to 'adjust' some of your favourite recipes.

This isn't a diet book, but a cookbook of wholesome family meals with reduced fat—delicious alternatives to buying pre-packed supermarket low-fat dinners, many of which tend to be bland, insubstantial and quite expensive. What we've done is taken a selection of popular recipes and looked at reducing their fat content. We certainly haven't wanted to compromise on taste, so if your personal favourite isn't included, it may be because it tastes so great the way it is that a low-fat version would be a poor substitute. Luckily, our spaghetti bolognese, lasagne, potato wedges and even fudgy chocolate brownies all passed the taste test.

Fat is often portrayed as a villain and we must remember that it is not—everyone needs a certain amount of fat in their body, to help with growth and development and to carry fat-soluble vitamins throughout the body. It is the quantity and type of fat we eat that can cause problems. Foods contain a mix of different fats, but one type usually predominates in each food.

Saturated fats, those that have been implicated in some health problems and can raise cholesterol levels, are found mainly in animal products, including butter, cream, fat on meat and other fats which are solid at room temperature, like dripping or lard.

Mono-unsaturated fats, which are generally regarded as being better for us, are found in olives, olive oil, many vegetable oils, most nuts, avocados and, in small amounts, in fish, chicken, lean meat and also eggs.

Polyunsaturated fats, found in nuts, grains, seeds and oily fish, usually remain soft at room temperature and also do not have the poor health implications of saturated fats.

However, although some fats are undoubtedly better for us than others, most tend to be high in calories. So if you are wanting to reduce the fat in your diet, don't eat too many nuts or avocados. If you are aiming to lose weight, cutting back on your fat intake is a good place to start and this book will certainly help you monitor that, but you do also need to consult your doctor and take advice about an exercise programme.

If you want to limit your fat intake, it is recommended you have no more than about 30–40 g of fat per day (30 g for women and small men, 40 g for men and taller women). With this in mind, we have developed recipes with the following amounts of fat per serve:

- Soups and starters with up to 8 g fat
- Main courses with up to 15 g fat
- Desserts with up to 8 g fat.

You will find a variety of recipes, from hearty family dinners to dishes suitable for entertaining. Eating low-fat doesn't mean missing out on anything.

HELPFUL INGREDIENTS

As well as using the recipes in this book, once you get used to cooking and eating the low-fat way, you will find you don't need to completely give up many of your favourite dishes but you can adapt them yourself by using lower-fat ingredients. There are simple ways to change your cooking habits and other ways will become obvious when you use the recipes. Try low-fat natural yoghurt instead of sour cream, or whipped ricotta with orange instead of whipped cream. Use fish canned in brine or spring water instead of oil. Buy chicken breast fillets that are sold without the skin, or remove the skin when you unpack them.

These days we are lucky with the choice and variety of low-fat foods available—dairy products such as cheese and spreads for bread, and meat which is sold well trimmed and labelled according to its fat content. The lean pre-trimmed cuts of meat (pork and lamb as well as beef) are excellent for making your own mince. Some shop-bought mince has quite a high proportion of fat, so make your own in a food processor. Avoid sausages, pies, pasties and burgers as these are made from poorer quality meat with higher proportions of fat. Eat more seafood, chicken and turkey (with the skin removed).

BETTER TIPS FOR BETTER EATING

- Trim all visible fat from meat or chicken, before and after cooking.
- Remove any chicken skin before cooking, to avoid the temptation to eat it when it's crispy and cooked.
- Use less meat in stews and casseroles. Instead, add lots of fresh vegetables or pulses such as chickpeas or kidney beans instead.
- Increase the amount of fish and legumes in your diet.
- Serve meals with plain pasta, boiled or dry-roasted potatoes or boiled/steamed rice to help you fill up with no extra added fats. Remember it's not the potato that contains the fat, but what goes on top.
- Skim stews or soups to remove excess fat or, better still, refrigerate overnight and lift off solidified fat. The flavour of most soups and stews is better after a day's refrigeration.
- Use low-fat plain or skim milk yoghurt in sauces and stews instead of cream.
- Thicken sauces by reducing the liquid and adding puréed vegetables, instead of making buttery sauces.
- Try alternatives to oil for basting and moistening (lemon or orange juice, vegetable juices, mustards, soy sauce, wine or fortified wines such as sherry). For tomato-based sauces such as bolognese, try frying onions in a little of the juice from tinned tomatoes.
- Use stock in soups instead of cream.
- Use light evaporated skim milk as a substitute for regular cream and light coconut milk instead of regular.
- Never go shopping when you're hungry and your resistance is low.

DON'T GO HUNGRY

Snack on low-fat, high fibre and no-fat foods between meals:

- Fresh fruit and vegetables (but not too much avocado).
- Fruit and vegetable juices.
- Skim milk and low-fat milk drinks; low-fat yoghurt.
- Pasta with tomato-based sauces.
- Steamed rice.
- Baked jacket potato with low-fat yoghurt and chives.
- Home-made muffins.
- Wholegrain bread and bread rolls; bagels; English muffins; crumpets with low-fat spread such as honey, jam or Marmite.
- Some crispbreads (read the labels).
- Rice cakes.
- Plain popcorn and baked pretzels.
- Dried fruit.

For those who love cheese, there are many fat-reduced Cheddars on the market but it is also worth knowing that other cheeses, such as feta and ricotta, have low-fat versions.

Read all the labels on food packaging. These will tell you how much fat is contained in a recommended serving size or in a 100 g portion. If there isn't a nutritional table on the packaging, the manufacturers must list the ingredients in order of the quantities used. If the fat is near the top of the list, try another brand.

Be aware that just because a product is labelled 'light', this doesn't necessarily mean light in fat: it can mean low in salt, flavour, colour and weight or low in alcohol. As well, don't be confused by foods claiming to be low-cholesterol or no-cholesterol—this doesn't necessarily mean low in fat—just low in animal fats. These foods, which may include nuts, nut products, margarines or oils, can still contain a high percentage of other fats. Processed foods tend to be higher in fat. The more natural and less prepared the food, the better it is for you.

LOW-FAT COOKING HINTS

Using a light spray of oil from an aerosol and a non-stick pan to cook will save many tablespoons of cooking oil over time. The aerosol cans simply contain oil under pressure; no chemicals have been added. Avoid deep-frying foods. In this book you will find occasional recipes for shallow-frying which don't break the 'fat-bank', but drain the food thoroughly on paper towels and enjoy these recipes in moderation.

Boiling, poaching and braising are all excellent ways to cook without adding fat. Steaming is a very good alternative to roasting, as it locks in the natural flavours. Add herbs, spices or lemon juice to meat, chicken or fish, or drizzle with sauce, then wrap in foil or baking paper and seal securely to keep in all the flavours. Steam in a bamboo or metal steamer, open the parcels at the table and enjoy the aroma and flavour. If you do roast joints of meat or poultry, place on a rack over a roasting tin so that the fat can collect below and be poured away. Once the meat is cooked, cut off any visible fat.

Stir-frying is a quick, healthy and relatively low-fat way to cook. This method uses a minimal amount of oil to seal meat and cooking is done quickly and at high temperatures so there is less opportunity for fat to be absorbed. The meat is then usually removed from the wok (it can be draining on paper towels) and set aside. When stir-frying vegetables, add a tablespoon of water to prevent them from sticking—this also produces steam which speeds up the cooking process even more. Return the meat to the pan, add any sauces and flavourings and toss well.

Grilling and barbecuing are not only low-fat but produce wonderful flavours. Lightly grease the grill or barbecue with oil spray or brush lightly with oil. If you grill on a rack, rather than a hotplate, fat can run off the meat. Try marinating or basting meat with orange juice, vinegar or yoghurt rather than oil. Chargrill pans, lightly brushed or sprayed with oil, are a good low-fat method of cooking.

soups & stews

CHICKEN AND VEGETABLE SOUP

Preparation time: 1 hour + refrigeration
Total cooking time: 1 hour 25 minutes
Serves 6–8

1.5 kg (3 lb) chicken
2 carrots, roughly chopped
2 celery sticks, roughly chopped
1 onion, quartered
4 fresh parsley sprigs
2 bay leaves
4 black peppercorns
50 g (1 3/4 oz) butter
2 tablespoons plain flour
2 potatoes, chopped
250 g (8 oz) butternut pumpkin, cut into bite-sized pieces
2 carrots, extra, cut into matchsticks
1 leek, cut into matchsticks
3 celery sticks, extra, cut into matchsticks
100 g (3 1/2 oz) green beans, cut into short lengths, or baby green beans, halved
200 g (6 1/2 oz) broccoli, cut into small florets
100 g (3 1/2 oz) sugar snap peas, trimmed
50 g (1 3/4 oz) English spinach leaves, shredded
1/2 cup (125 ml/4 fl oz) cream
1/4 cup (15 g/1/2 oz) chopped fresh parsley

1 Place the chicken in a large pan with the carrot, celery, onion, parsley, bay leaves, 2 teaspoons of salt and the peppercorns. Add 3 litres of water. Bring to the boil, then reduce the heat and simmer for 1 hour, skimming the surface as required. Allow to cool for at least 30 minutes. Strain and reserve the liquid.

2 Remove the chicken and allow to cool until it is cool enough to handle. Discard the skin, then cut or pull the flesh from the bones and shred into small pieces. Set the chicken meat aside.

3 Heat the butter in a large pan over medium heat and, when foaming, add the flour. Cook, stirring, for 1 minute. Remove from the heat and gradually stir in the stock. Return to the heat and bring to the boil, stirring constantly. Add the potato, pumpkin and extra carrot and simmer for 7 minutes. Add the leek, extra celery and beans and simmer for a further 5 minutes. Finally, add the broccoli and sugar snap peas and cook for a further 3 minutes.

4 Just before serving, add the chicken, spinach, cream and chopped parsley. Reheat gently but do not allow the soup to boil. Keep stirring until the spinach has wilted. Season to taste with salt and freshly ground black pepper. Serve the soup immediately.

NUTRITION PER SERVE (8)
Protein 50 g; Fat 15 g; Carbohydrate 15 g; Dietary Fibre 6 g; Cholesterol 130 mg; 1700 kJ (400 Cal)

HINT: Do not overcook the vegetables. They should be tender yet crispy.

NOTE: The chicken stock (up to the end of Step 1) can be made 1 day ahead and kept, covered, in the refrigerator. This can, in fact, be beneficial—before reheating the stock, spoon off the fat which will have formed on the surface.

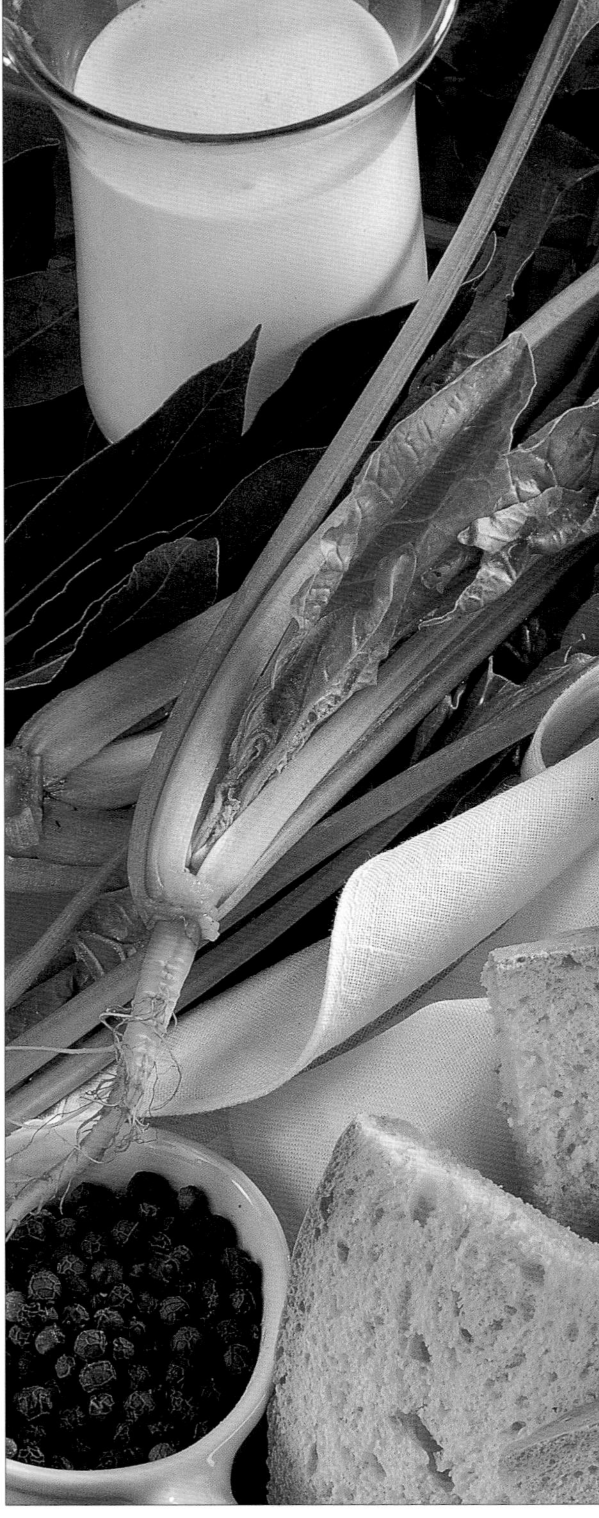

Cut the extra celery into short lengths, then into matchsticks.

Using a knife, trim the tops from the sugar snap peas, pulling down to remove the string.

Add the parsley sprigs and bay leaves to the chicken and vegetables in the pan.

Remove the skin from the cooled chicken, then shred the meat.

Add the potato, pumpkin and extra carrot to the boiling soup.

Pour in the cream and stir until the spinach has just wilted.

LAMB AND PASTA SOUP

Preparation time: 10 minutes
Total cooking time: 40 minutes
Serves 6–8

2 tablespoons oil
500 g (1 lb) lean lamb meat, cut into bite-sized cubes
2 onions, finely chopped
2 carrots, chopped
4 celery stalks, chopped
425 g (14 oz) can crushed tomatoes
2 litres beef stock
300 g (10 oz) spiral pasta
chopped fresh parsley, for serving

1 Heat the oil in a large pan and cook the lamb in batches until golden brown. Remove each batch as it is cooked and drain on paper towels. Add the onion to the pan and cook for 2 minutes or until softened. Return all the meat to the pan.
2 Add the carrot, celery, tomato and beef stock. Stir to combine and bring to the boil. Reduce the heat to low and simmer, covered, for 15 minutes.
3 Add the spiral pasta to the soup. Stir briefly to prevent the pasta sticking to the pan. Simmer, uncovered, for another 15 minutes or until the lamb and pasta are tender. Sprinkle with chopped parsley before serving.

NUTRITION PER SERVE (8):
Protein 20 g; Fat 8 g; Carbohydrate 34 g; Dietary Fibre 4 g; Cholesterol 41 mg; 1195 kJ (285 cal)

STORAGE: This soup can be kept, covered, in the fridge for up to 3 days.
HINT: The pasta can be cooked separately, drained and added to the soup just before serving.
VARIATIONS: For a lighter flavour, use half stock and half water. Vegetable stock can be used instead of beef.

Cook the lamb in batches so that it browns without stewing.

Add the carrot and celery, tomatoes and beef stock to the pan.

Add the spiral pasta to the soup and stir briefly to prevent it sticking.

LEEK AND POTATO SOUP

Preparation time: 20 minutes
Total cooking time: 45 minutes
Serves 4

cooking oil spray
2 leeks, white part only, sliced
3 cloves garlic, crushed
1 teaspoon ground cumin
1 kg (2 lb) potatoes, chopped
1.25 litres vegetable stock
1/2 cup (125 ml/4 fl oz) skim milk

1 Lightly spray a large non-stick frying pan with oil. Add the leek, garlic and 1 tablespoon water to prevent sticking, then cook over low heat, stirring frequently, for 25 minutes, or until the leek turns lightly golden. Add the ground cumin and cook for a further 2 minutes.
2 Put the potato in a large pan with the leek mixture and stock, bring to the boil, reduce the heat and simmer for 10–15 minutes, or until tender. Purée in a processor or blender until smooth. Return to the pan.
3 Stir in the milk, season and heat through before serving.

NUTRITION PER SERVE
Protein 8 g; Fat 1 g; Carbohydrate 35 g; Dietary Fibre 5.5 g; Cholesterol 1 mg; 795 kJ (190 Cal)

Stir the leek and garlic over low heat for about 25 minutes, until golden.

Add the cooked leek mixture to the chopped potato and stock.

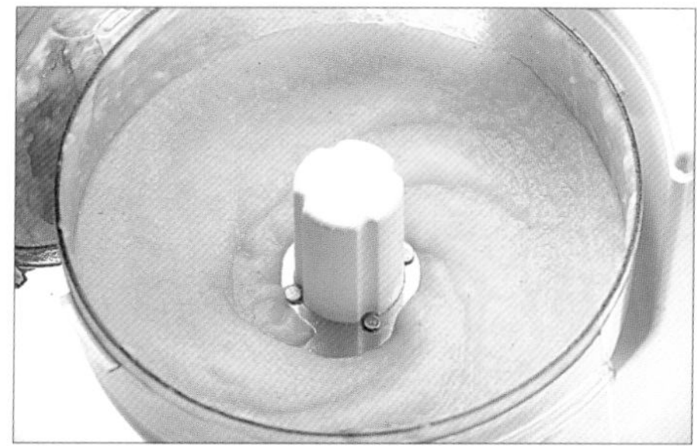
Purée the soup in a food processor or blender, in batches if necessary.

CURRIED SWEET POTATO SOUP

Preparation time: 20 minutes
Total cooking time: 40 minutes
Serves 6

- 1 tablespoon oil
- 1 large onion, chopped
- 2 cloves garlic, crushed
- 3 teaspoons curry powder
- 1.25 kg (2 lb 8 oz) orange sweet potato, peeled and cubed
- 4 cups (1 litre) chicken stock
- 1 large apple, peeled, cored and grated
- 1/2 cup (125 ml/4 fl oz) light coconut milk

1 Heat the oil in a large pan over medium heat and cook the onion for 10 minutes, stirring occasionally, until very soft. Add the garlic and curry powder and cook for a minute further.
2 Add the sweet potato, stock and apple. Bring to the boil, reduce the heat and simmer, partially covered, for 30 minutes, until very soft.
3 Cool the soup a little before processing in batches until smooth. Return to the pan, stir in the coconut milk and reheat gently without boiling. Serve with warm pitta bread.

NUTRITION PER SERVE
Protein 5 g; Fat 8 g; Carbohydrate 35 g; Dietary Fibre 5.5 g; Cholesterol 0 mg; 975 kJ (233 cal)

STORAGE TIME: Can be kept in the fridge for 1 day without the coconut milk: add this when you reheat.

HINT: The soup will become quite thick on standing. Thin with stock or water if necessary.

Add the garlic and curry powder to the softened onion and cook for another minute.

Stir in the stock with the cubed sweet potato and grated apple.

Once the soup has been processed stir in the coconut milk.

LEMON CHILLI CHICKEN

Preparation time: 20 minutes
Total cooking time: 35 minutes
Serves 4

2 garlic cloves, chopped
1 tablespoon grated fresh ginger
2 tablespoons olive oil
600 g (1 1/4 lb) chicken thigh fillets
1 teaspoon ground coriander
2 teaspoons ground cumin
1/2 teaspoon ground turmeric
1 red chilli, chopped
1/2 cup (125 ml/4 fl oz) lemon juice
3/4 cup (185 ml/6 fl oz) white wine
1 cup (30 g/1 oz) fresh coriander leaves

1 Blend the garlic, ginger and 1 tablespoon water into a paste in a small food processor or mortar and pestle. Heat the olive oil in a heavy-based pan and brown the chicken in batches. Remove with a slotted spoon and set aside.

2 Add the garlic paste to the pan and cook, stirring, for 1 minute. Add the coriander, cumin, turmeric and chilli and stir-fry for 1 minute more. Stir in the lemon juice and wine.

3 Add the chicken pieces to the pan and stir to combine. Bring to the boil, then reduce the heat, cover and cook, stirring, for about 20–25 minutes, or until the chicken is tender. Remove the lid and cook the sauce over high heat for 5 minutes to reduce it by half. Stir in the coriander and season with salt and pepper to taste. Serve on a bed of steamed jasmine rice.

NUTRITION PER SERVE
Protein 30 g; Fat 15 g; Carbohydrate 0 g; Dietary Fibre 0 g; Cholesterol 105 mg; 1290 kJ (310 cal)

Brown the chicken in batches to stop the meat from stewing.

Add the coriander, cumin, turmeric and chilli and stir-fry for 1 minute.

Once the sauce has reduced, stir in the fresh coriander leaves.

SCOTCH BROTH

Preparation time: 20 minutes
Total cooking time: 2 1/2 hours
Serves 10

750 g (1 1/2 lb) neck lamb chops or lamb shanks
250 g (8 oz) pearl barley or soup mix (see NOTE)
1 carrot, peeled and diced
1 turnip, peeled and diced
1 parsnip, peeled and diced
1 onion, finely chopped
1 small leek, thinly sliced
1 cup (75 g/2 1/2 oz) shredded cabbage
1/2 cup (15 g/1/2 oz) chopped parsley

1 Cut away any excess fat from the meat. Put the meat in a large heavy-based pan with 10 cups (2 1/2 litres) water. Bring to the boil, reduce the heat and simmer, covered, for 1 hour. Skim any froth from the surface frequently. Meanwhile, soak the pearl barley or soup mix in a large bowl of water for about 1 hour.
2 Add the carrot, turnip, parsnip, onion and leek to the pan. Drain the barley or soup mix and add to the pan. Stir well to combine, cover and simmer for a further 1 1/2 hours. Stir in the cabbage 10 minutes before the end of cooking time. (Add more water at this stage if you like a thinner soup.)
3 Remove the meat from the pan using tongs. Leave to cool before removing the meat from the bones. Chop the meat finely and return it to the soup. Add parsley and season with salt and pepper.

NUTRITION PER SERVE
Protein 21 g; Fat 2 g; Carbohydrate 20 g; Dietary Fibre 4 g; Cholesterol 50 mg; 750 kJ (180 cal)

STORAGE TIME: May be kept covered and refrigerated for up to 3 days. Suitable to freeze up to 1 month.

NOTE: Soup mix is a combination of pearl barley, split peas and lentils. Both pearl barley and soup mix are readily available from supermarkets.

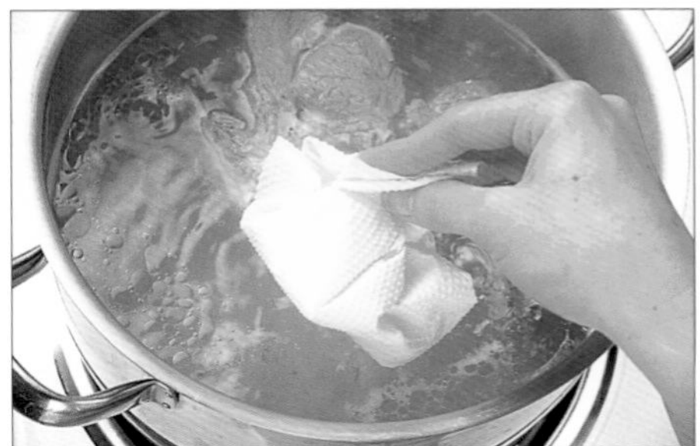

Instead of a spoon, use paper towels to skim any froth from the surface.

Drain the barley or soup mix and add to the pan of simmering meat and vegetables.

Use tongs to lift the bones out of the soup and then cut the meat from the bones.

PORK STEW WITH ASIAN FLAVOURS

Preparation time: 20 minutes
Total cooking time: 50 minutes
Serves 4

2 teaspoons olive oil
2 cloves garlic, crushed
1 tablespoon julienned fresh ginger
1 teaspoon Sichuan pepper, crushed
1 star anise
800 g (1 lb 10 oz) pork fillet, cut into 3 cm (1 1/4 inch) cubes
1 cup (250 ml/8 fl oz) chicken stock
1 tablespoon light soy sauce
1 tablespoon cornflour
2 teaspoons chilli bean paste
250 g (8 oz) Chinese broccoli, cut into 4 cm (1 1/2 inch) lengths

1 Heat the olive oil in a heavy-based saucepan over high heat. Add the garlic, ginger, Sichuan pepper and star anise and cook for 30 seconds, or until fragrant. Stir in the pork to coat.
2 Add the stock, soy sauce and 1 cup (250 ml/8 fl oz) water to the pan and bring to the boil. Reduce the heat and simmer for 40 minutes, or until the pork is tender. Combine the cornflour with 2 tablespoons of the cooking liquid, stirring until smooth. Add to the pan and stir over medium heat for 3–4 minutes, or until the mixture thickens slightly.
3 Stir in the bean paste and Chinese broccoli and cook for a further 2 minutes, or until the broccoli is just tender. Serve with steamed rice.

NUTRITION PER SERVE
Protein 47 g; Fat 7 g; Carbohydrate 4 g; Dietary Fibre 3 g; Cholesterol 190 mg; 1135 kJ (270 Cal)

Crush the Sichuan pepper in a mortar and pestle before heating it with the other spices.

Cut the Chinese broccoli into 4 cm (1 1/2 inch) lengths, using a sharp knife.

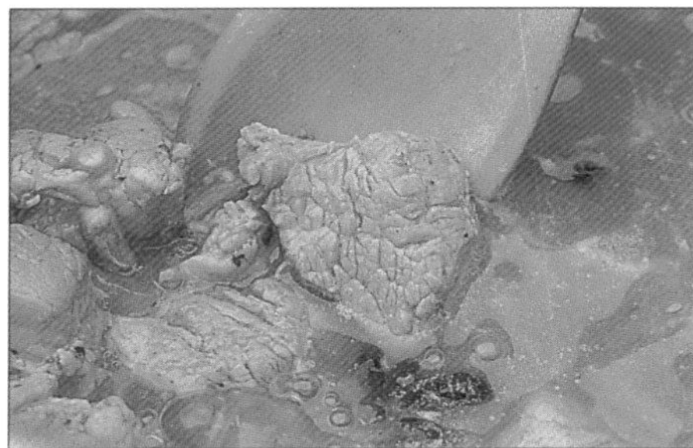
Stir the cornflour mixture into the stew until the mixture thickens slightly.

SPICY CHICKEN BROTH WITH CORIANDER PASTA

Preparation time: 40 minutes
Total cooking time: 50 minutes
Serves 4

350 g (11 oz) chicken thighs or wings, skin removed
2 carrots, finely chopped
2 celery stalks, finely chopped
2 small leeks, finely chopped
3 egg whites
6 cups chicken stock
Tabasco sauce

CORIANDER PASTA
1/2 cup (60 g/2 oz) plain flour
1 egg
1/2 teaspoon sesame oil
small bunch fresh coriander leaves

1 Put the chicken pieces, carrot, celery and leek in a large heavy-based pan. Push the chicken to one side and add the egg whites to the vegetables. Using a wire whisk, beat for a minute or so until frothy (take care not to use a pan that can be scratched by the whisk).
2 Warm the stock in another pan, then add gradually to the first pan, whisking continuously to froth the egg whites. Continue whisking while slowly bringing to the boil. Make a hole in the froth on top with a spoon and leave to simmer, uncovered, for 30 minutes without stirring.
3 Line a large strainer with a damp tea towel or double thickness of muslin and strain the broth into a clean bowl (discard the chicken and vegetables). Season with salt, pepper and Tabasco to taste. Set aside.
4 To make the coriander pasta, sift the flour into a bowl and make a well in the centre. Whisk the egg and oil together and pour into the well. Mix together to make a soft pasta dough and knead on a lightly floured surface for 2 minutes, until smooth.
5 Divide the pasta dough into four even portions. Roll one portion out very thinly and cover with a layer of evenly spaced coriander leaves. Roll out another portion of pasta and lay this on top of the leaves, then gently roll the layers together. Repeat with the remaining pasta and coriander.
6 Cut out squares of pasta around the leaves. The pasta may then be left to sit and dry out if it is not needed immediately. When you are ready to serve, heat the chicken broth gently in a saucepan. As the broth simmers, add the pasta and cook for 1 minute. Serve immediately.

NUTRITION PER SERVE
Protein 25 g; Fat 4 g; Carbohydrate 18 g; Dietary Fibre 4 g; Cholesterol 90 mg; 915 kJ (220 cal)

HINT: Beg, borrow or steal a pasta machine for making this fine, delicate pasta. A rolling pin will suffice if necessary but you will need to roll the pasta as thinly as possible.
NOTE: The egg whites added to the vegetable and chicken stock pot make the broth very clear rather than leaving it with the normal cloudy appearance of chicken stock. This is called clarifying the stock. When you strain the broth through muslin or a tea towel, don't press the solids to extract the extra liquid or the broth will become cloudy. It is necessary to make a hole in the froth on top to prevent the stock boiling over.

Use a wire whisk to beat the egg white and vegetables.

Use a metal spoon to make a hole in the froth on top of the soup.

Strain the broth through a damp tea towel or double thickness of muslin.

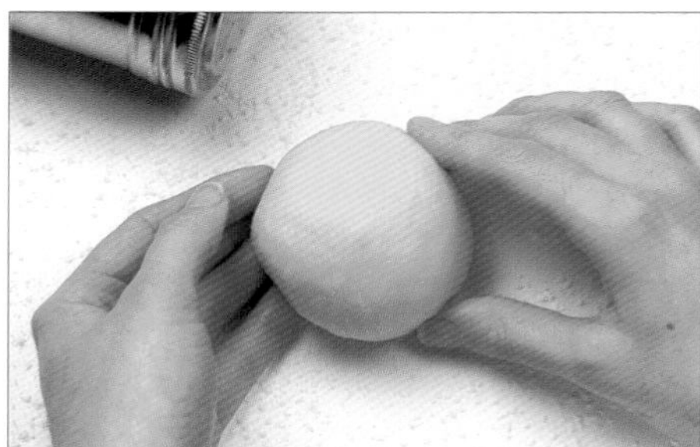
Knead the dough on a lightly floured surface until it is smooth.

Lay a second layer of thin pasta over the coriander leaves.

Cut out neat squares of pasta around each coriander leaf.

HERBED CHICKEN SOUP

Preparation time: 30 minutes
Total cooking time: 30 minutes
Serves 6

1 chicken breast fillet
1 bay leaf
6 black peppercorns
1 whole clove
4 fresh parsley sprigs
2 tablespoons olive oil
1 onion, finely chopped
1 small carrot, finely chopped
1 celery stick, finely chopped
1 large potato, finely chopped
1 teaspoon finely chopped fresh rosemary, or 1/4 teaspoon dried
1 teaspoon chopped fresh thyme, or 1/2 teaspoon dried
1 teaspoon chopped fresh marjoram, or 1/2 teaspoon dried
1 litre chicken stock
310 g (10 oz) can creamed corn
1/4 cup (15 g/1/2 oz) finely chopped fresh parsley

1 Trim the chicken breast of excess fat and sinew. Put 2 cups (500 ml/16 fl oz) water in a pan and bring to a simmer. Add the chicken, bay leaf, peppercorns, clove and parsley and cook for 5 minutes, or until the chicken is tender. Remove the chicken from the liquid and cool slightly before shredding. Discard the bay leaf, peppercorns, clove and parsley, and reserve the cooking liquid.

2 Heat the oil in a large, heavy-based pan. Add the onion, carrot and celery and cook over medium heat for 5 minutes, or until the onion is soft. Add the potato, rosemary, thyme and marjoram and cook, stirring, over medium heat for 1 minute.

3 Add the stock and reserved cooking liquid. Season with salt and pepper and bring to the boil. Reduce the heat and simmer for 15 minutes, or until the potato and carrot have softened. Add the creamed corn and shredded chicken and stir for 2 minutes, or until heated through. Stir in the parsley.

NUTRITION PER SERVE
Protein 11 g; Fat 7.5 g; Carbohydrate 15 g; Dietary Fibre 3 g; Cholesterol 18 mg; 695 kJ (166 cal)

HINT: Use shredded barbecued chicken if you prefer—add extra stock to make up the liquid.

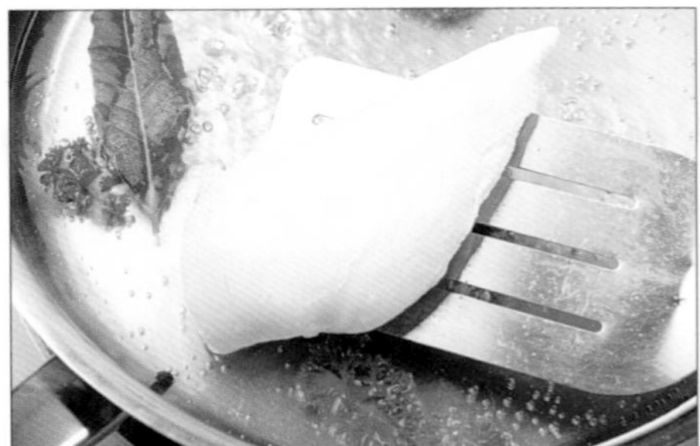

Simmer the chicken breast with the bay leaf, peppercorns, clove and parsley until tender.

Add the potato and herbs to the vegetable mixture and cook over medium heat.

Add the shredded chicken and creamed corn to the soup.

BEAN AND CAPSICUM STEW

Preparation time: 20 minutes + overnight soaking
Total cooking time: 1 hour 35 minutes
Serves 4–6

- 1 cup (200 g/$6^{1}/_{2}$ oz) dried haricot beans (see NOTE)
- 2 tablespoons olive oil
- 2 large cloves garlic, crushed
- 1 red onion, halved and cut into thin wedges
- 1 red capsicum, cubed
- 1 green capsicum, cubed
- 2 x 400 g (13 oz) cans chopped tomatoes
- 2 tablespoons tomato paste
- 2 cups (500 ml/16 fl oz) vegetable stock
- 2 tablespoons chopped fresh basil
- $^{2}/_{3}$ cup (125 g/4 oz) Kalamata olives, pitted
- 1–2 teaspoons soft brown sugar

1 Put the beans in a large bowl, cover with cold water and soak overnight. Rinse well, then transfer to a saucepan, cover with cold water and cook for 45 minutes, or until just tender. Drain.
2 Heat the oil in a large saucepan. Cook the garlic and onion over medium heat for 2–3 minutes, or until the onion is soft. Add the red and green capsicums and cook for a further 5 minutes.
3 Stir in the tomato, tomato paste, stock and beans. Simmer, covered, for 40 minutes, or until the beans are cooked through. Stir in the basil, olives and sugar. Season with salt and pepper. Serve hot with crusty bread.

NUTRITION PER SERVE (6)
Protein 10 g; Fat 8 g; Carbohydrate 20 g; Dietary Fibre 9.5 g; Cholesterol 0 mg; 825 kJ (197 cal)

NOTE: 1 cup of dried haricot beans yields about $2^{1}/_{2}$ cups cooked beans. So use $2^{1}/_{2}$ cups tinned haricot or borlotti beans instead if you prefer.

Cook the garlic and onion until the garlic is soft, then add the capsicum.

Simmer the stew for 40 minutes, or until the beans are cooked through.

CYPRIOT PORK AND CORIANDER STEW

Preparation time: 15 minutes
+ overnight marinating
Total cooking time:
1 hour 20 minutes
Serves 4–6

1 1/2 tablespoons coriander seeds
800 g (1 lb 10 oz) pork fillet, cut into 2 cm (3/4 inch) dice
1 tablespoon plain flour
1/4 cup (60 ml/2 fl oz) olive oil
1 large onion, thinly sliced
1 1/2 cups (375 ml/12 fl oz) red wine
1 cup (250 ml/8 fl oz) chicken stock
1 teaspoon sugar
fresh coriander sprigs, to garnish

1 Crush the coriander seeds in a mortar and pestle. Combine the pork, crushed seeds and 1/2 teaspoon cracked pepper in a bowl. Cover and marinate overnight in the fridge.
2 Combine the flour and pork and toss. Heat 2 tablespoons oil in a frying pan and cook the pork in batches over high heat for 1–2 minutes, or until brown. Remove.
3 Heat the remaining oil, add the onion and cook over medium heat for 2–3 minutes, or until just golden. Return the meat to the pan, add the red wine, stock and sugar, and season. Bring to the boil, then reduce the heat and simmer, covered, for 1 hour.
4 Remove the meat. Return the pan to the heat and boil over high heat for 3–5 minutes, or until reduced and slightly thickened. Pour over the meat and top with the coriander.

NUTRITION PER SERVE (6)
Protein 30 g; Fat 12 g; Carbohydrate 2.5 g; Dietary Fibre 0 g; Cholesterol 65 mg; 1180 kJ (282 Cal)

Coat the pork fillet pieces in the ground coriander and pepper.

Heat some oil in a frying pan and cook the pork in batches until brown.

Remove the meat from the pan and keep warm while making the sauce.

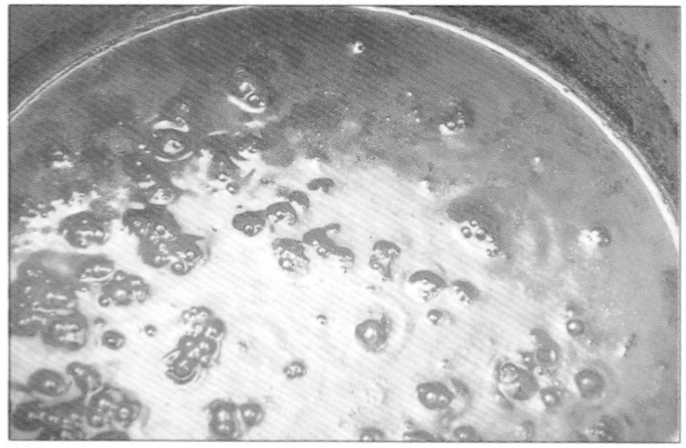

Boil the liquid until reduced and slightly thickened.

LEMON-SCENTED BROTH WITH TORTELLINI

Preparation time: 10 minutes
Total cooking time: 20 minutes
Serves 4–6

1 lemon
1/2 cup (125 ml/4 fl oz) white wine
440 g (14 oz) can chicken consommé
1/3 cup (20 g/3/4 oz) chopped fresh parsley
375 g (12 oz) fresh or dried veal- or chicken-filled tortellini

1 Using a vegetable peeler, peel wide strips from the lemon. Remove the white pith with a small sharp knife and cut three of the wide pieces into fine strips. Set these aside for garnishing.
2 Place the wide lemon strips, white wine, consommé and 3 cups (750 ml/ 24 fl oz) water in a large deep pan. Cook for 10 minutes over low heat. Remove the lemon rind and bring to the boil.
3 Add half the parsley, the tortellini and a sprinkling of black pepper to the pan. Cook for 6–7 minutes or until the pasta is *al dente*. Garnish with the remaining parsley and the fine strips of lemon.

NUTRITION PER SERVE (6)
Protein 6 g; Fat 4 g; Carbohydrate 9 g; Dietary Fibre 2 g; Cholesterol 14 mg; 483 kJ (115 cal)

STORAGE: If you want, you can prepare the recipe up to the end of step 2 and then leave in the fridge for a day before adding the pasta.

Remove wide strips of peel from the lemon and then remove the bitter white pith.

Cook for 10 minutes and then lift out the strips of lemon with a slotted spoon.

Bring the liquid to the boil and then add the parsley and tortellini.

TOMATO AND POTATO STEW

Preparation time: 30 minutes
Total cooking time: 1 hour 15 minutes
Serves 6

1/4 cup (60 ml/2 fl oz) olive oil
2 red capsicums, chopped
2 green capsicums, chopped
3 onions, thinly sliced
4 cloves garlic, crushed
2 x 400 g (13 oz) cans chopped tomatoes
3–4 sprigs thyme, plus extra to garnish
2 bay leaves
2 teaspoons caster sugar
1.2 kg (2 lb 7 oz) potatoes, cut into chunks
1 cup (125 g/4 oz) black olives, pitted
Parmesan shavings, to serve

1 Heat the oil in a large, heavy-based pan. When the oil is hot, cook the capsicum, onion and garlic over medium heat for 10 minutes, or until softened. Add the chopped tomatoes, 125 ml (4 fl oz) water, thyme sprigs, bay leaves and sugar. Season with salt and pepper to taste and leave to simmer gently for 15 minutes.
2 Add the potato chunks, cover and cook very gently for about an hour, or until tender. Stir in the olives. Garnish with Parmesan shavings and thyme.

NUTRITION PER SERVE
Protein 10 g; Fat 12 g; Carbohydrate 40 g; Dietary Fibre 9 g; Cholesterol 3 mg; 1330 kJ (320 cal)

When the oil is hot, fry the capsicum, onion and garlic until soft.

Add the chunks of potato to the tomato mixture and cook very gently until tender.

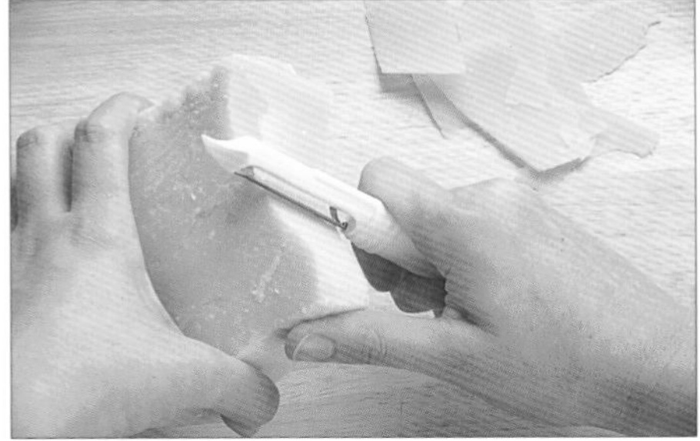

The easiest way to make Parmesan shavings is to run a vegetable peeler over the block.

SPICY GARLIC CHICKEN

Preparation time: 30 minutes
Total cooking time: 1 hour
Serves 4–6

1.4 kg (2 lb 13 oz) chicken
1 small bunch coriander
2 tablespoons olive oil
4 cloves garlic, crushed
2 red onions, thinly sliced
1 large red capsicum, cut into squares
1 teaspoon ground ginger
1 teaspoon chilli powder
1 teaspoon caraway seeds, crushed
1 teaspoon ground turmeric
2 teaspoons ground coriander
2 teaspoons ground cumin
1/2 cup (60 g/2 oz) raisins
1/2 cup (90 g/3 oz) black olives
1 teaspoon finely grated lemon rind

1 Trim the chicken of excess fat and sinew. Cut the chicken into 12 serving pieces. Finely chop the coriander roots, reserving the leaves.
2 Heat the oil in a large heavy-based pan. Add the garlic, onion, capsicum, ginger, chilli powder, caraway seeds, turmeric, coriander, cumin and coriander roots. Cook over medium heat for 10 minutes.
3 Add the chicken pieces and stir until combined. Add 1 1/2 cups (375 ml/12 fl oz) water and bring to the boil. Reduce the heat and simmer for 45 minutes, or until the chicken is tender and cooked through.
4 Add the raisins, black olives and lemon rind and simmer for a further 5 minutes. Serve with pasta or rice. May be served sprinkled with the reserved coriander leaves.

NUTRITION PER SERVE
Protein 33 g; Fat 13 g; Carbohydrate 13 g; Dietary Fibre 2 g; Cholesterol 105 mg; 1236 kJ (295 cal)

VARIATION: Chicken pieces may be used instead of whole chicken.

Wash the coriander and finely chop the roots, reserving the leaves.

Heat the oil in a large pan and add the garlic, onion, capsicum and spices.

Add the chicken pieces to the mixture and stir until combined.

Add the raisins, olives and lemon rind to the chicken mixture.

GAZPACHO

Preparation time: 40 minutes + 3 hours refrigeration
Total cooking time: Nil
Serves 4–6

750 g (1 1/2 lb) ripe tomatoes
1 Lebanese cucumber, chopped
1 green capsicum, chopped
2–3 cloves garlic, crushed
1–2 tablespoons finely chopped black olives
1/3 cup (80 ml/2 3/4 fl oz) red or white wine vinegar
1/4 cup (60 ml/2 fl oz) olive oil
1 tablespoon tomato paste

ACCOMPANIMENTS
1 onion, finely chopped
1 red capsicum, finely chopped
2 spring onions, finely chopped
1 Lebanese cucumber, finely chopped
2 hard-boiled eggs, chopped
chopped fresh mint or parsley
croutons

1 To peel the tomatoes, score a cross in the base of each tomato. Cover with boiling water for 30 seconds, then plunge into cold water. Drain and peel away the tomato skin from the cross. Chop the flesh so finely that it is almost a purée.
2 Mix together the tomato, cucumber, capsicum, garlic, olives, vinegar, oil,

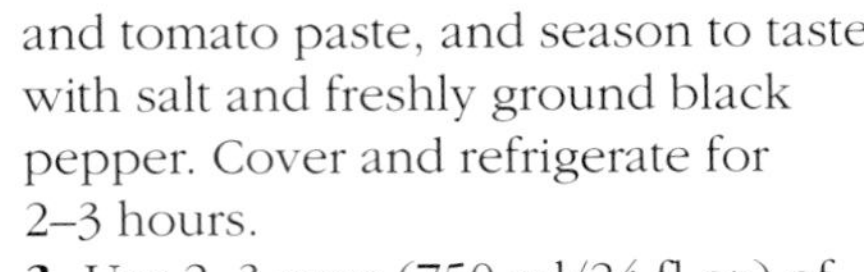

and tomato paste, and season to taste with salt and freshly ground black pepper. Cover and refrigerate for 2–3 hours.
3 Use 2–3 cups (750 ml/24 fl oz) of chilled water to thin the soup to your taste. Serve chilled, with the chopped onion, capsicum, spring onion, cucumber, boiled egg, herbs and croutons served separately for diners to add to their own bowls.

NUTRITION PER SERVE (6)
Protein 5 g; Fat 2 g; Carbohydrate 7 g; Dietary Fibre 4 g; Cholesterol 70 mg; 310 kJ (75 cal)

Halve the cucumber lengthways, cut into strips and chop finely.

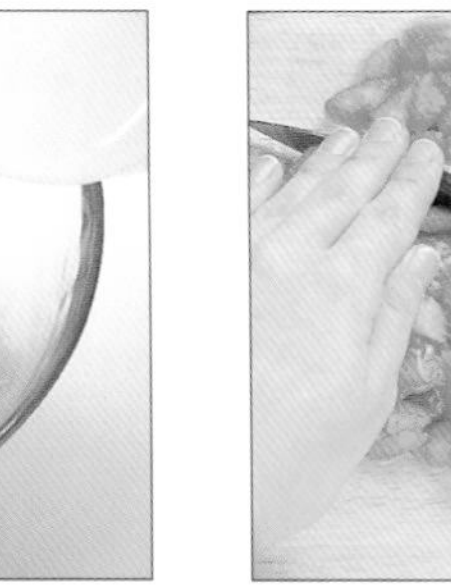

Put the tomatoes in a heatproof bowl and cover with boiling water.

Using a sharp knife, chop the tomato flesh very finely to a purée.

LENTIL AND SPINACH SOUP

Preparation time: 25 minutes
Total cooking time: 1 hour
Serves 8

1/2 cup (95 g/3 oz) brown lentils
2 tablespoons vegetable oil
1 leek, chopped
1 onion, chopped
1 stick celery, chopped
600 g (1 1/4 lb) potatoes, chopped
4 cups (1 litre/32 fl oz) vegetable stock
250 g (8 oz) English spinach

1 Put the lentils in a pan. Cover with water and bring to the boil, reduce the heat and simmer for 20 minutes, or until tender; drain.
2 Heat the oil in a large pan. Cook the leek, onion and celery for 5 minutes, or until softened. Add the potato and cook, stirring frequently, for 10 minutes. Add the vegetable stock and bring to the boil. Reduce the heat and simmer, covered, for 20 minutes, or until the potato is tender.
3 Remove the stalks from the spinach, wash the leaves well, add to the soup and cook for 1–2 minutes. Let the soup cool for a couple of minutes, then purée in a food processor or blender. Return to the pan, add the lentils and reheat gently before serving.

NUTRITION PER SERVE
Protein 5 g; Fat 5 g; Carbohydrate 15 g; Dietary Fibre 4 g; Cholesterol 0 mg; 505 kJ (120 cal)

Place the lentils in a pan and cover with plenty of cold water.

Cook the leek, onion and celery until soft, then add the chopped potato.

Add the cooked and drained lentils to the puréed soup in the pan.

CHICKEN AND ORANGE STEW

Preparation time: 50 minutes
Total cooking time: 1 hour 30 minutes
Serves 4–6

2 small chickens
1 tablespoon olive oil
2 thick slices bacon, rind removed and thinly sliced
50 g (1 3/4 oz) butter
16 small pickling onions, peeled, ends left intact
2–3 cloves garlic, crushed
3 teaspoons grated fresh ginger
2 teaspoons grated orange rind
2 teaspoons ground cumin
2 teaspoons ground coriander
2 tablespoons honey
1 cup (250 ml/8 fl oz) fresh orange juice
1 cup (250 ml/8 fl oz) white wine
1/2 cup (125 ml/4 fl oz) chicken or vegetable stock
1 bunch baby carrots
1 large parsnip, peeled
fresh coriander and orange zest, to serve

1 Using a sharp knife or a pair of kitchen scissors, cut each chicken into 8 pieces, discarding the backbone. Remove any excess fat and discard (remove the skin as well, if preferred).
2 Heat about a teaspoon of the oil in a large, deep, heavy-based pan. Add the bacon and cook over medium heat for 2–3 minutes or until just crisp. Remove from the pan and set aside to drain on paper towels. Add the remaining oil and half the butter to the pan. Cook the onions over medium heat until dark golden brown. Shake the pan occasionally to ensure even cooking and browning. Remove from the pan and set aside.
3 Add the chicken pieces to the pan and brown in small batches over medium heat. Remove from the pan and drain on paper towels.
4 Add the remaining butter to the pan. Stir in the garlic, ginger, orange rind, cumin, coriander and honey, and cook, stirring, for 1 minute. Add the orange juice, wine and stock to the pan. Bring to the boil, then reduce the heat and simmer for 1 minute. Return the chicken pieces to the pan, cover and leave to simmer over low heat for 40 minutes.
5 Return the onions and bacon to the pan and simmer, covered, for a further 15 minutes. Remove the lid and leave to simmer for a further 15 minutes.
6 Trim the carrots, leaving a little green stalk, and wash well or peel if necessary. Cut the parsnip into small batons. Add the carrots and parsnip to the pan. Cover and cook for 5–10 minutes, or until the carrots and parsnip are just tender. Do not overcook the carrots or they will lose their bright colouring. When you are ready to serve, arrange 2–3 chicken pieces on each plate. Arrange a couple of carrots and a few parsnip batons with the chicken and spoon a little sauce over the top. Garnish with the coriander leaves and orange zest.

NUTRITION PER SERVE
Protein 42 g; Fat 12 g; Carbohydrate 22 g; Dietary Fibre 2 g; Cholesterol 135 mg; 1635 kJ (395 cal)

Cut each chicken into 8 pieces using a knife or pair of scissors.

Cook the pickling onions in the oil and butter until they are dark golden brown.

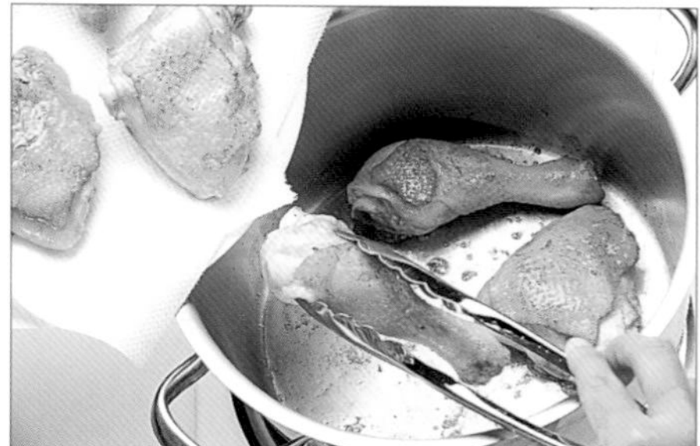

Brown the chicken pieces in batches and drain on paper towels.

Add the orange juice, white wine and stock to the pan, and bring to the boil.

Return the browned pickling onions and cooked bacon to the pan.

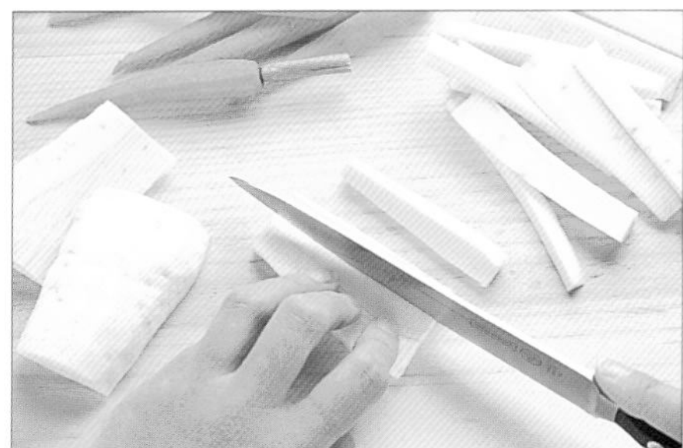
Cut the parsnip into batons and leave the stalks on the carrots to provide colour.

CHICKEN ADOBO

Preparation time: 20 minutes + 2 hours marinating
Total cooking time: 1 hour
Serves 6

1.5 kg (3 lb) chicken pieces
6 cloves garlic, crushed
1 cup (250 ml/8 fl oz) cider vinegar
1 1/2 cups (375 ml/12 fl oz) chicken stock
1 bay leaf
1 teaspoon coriander seeds
1 teaspoon black peppercorns
1/4 cup (60 ml/2 fl oz) soy sauce
1 teaspoon annatto seeds or 1/4 teaspoon paprika and 1/8 teaspoon turmeric
2 tablespoons oil

1 Combine all the ingredients, except the oil, in a large bowl. Cover and refrigerate for 2 hours.
2 Transfer the mixture to a large heavy-based pan and bring to the boil over high heat. Reduce the heat and simmer, covered, for 30 minutes. Uncover the pan and continue cooking for 10 minutes, or until the chicken is tender. Remove the chicken from the pan and set aside. Bring the liquid back to the boil and cook over high heat for 10 minutes, or until reduced by half.
3 Heat the oil in a wok or large non-stick frying pan and add the chicken in batches, cooking over medium heat for 5 minutes, or until crisp and golden. Serve the reduced sauce mixture over the chicken pieces and accompany with rice.

NUTRITION PER SERVE
Protein 38 g; Fat 10 g; Carbohydrate 0.5 g; Dietary Fibre 0.5 g; Cholesterol 83 mg; 1070 kJ (256 cal)

NOTE: Annatto seeds are available at speciality stores.

Mix the chicken with the marinade and refrigerate, covered, for 2 hours.

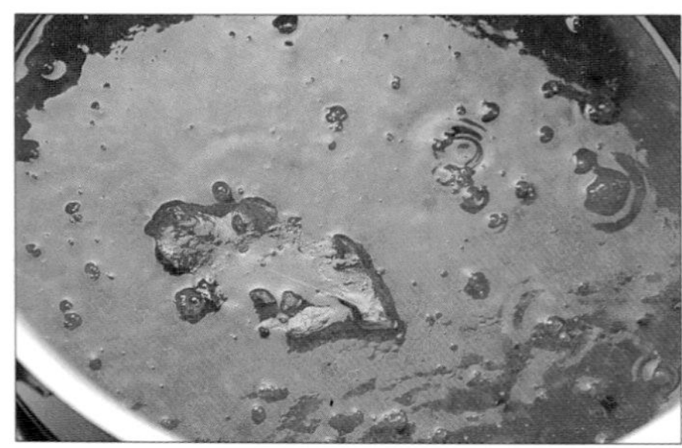
After removing the chicken from the pan, boil the liquid until it has reduced by half.

Cook the chicken pieces, in batches, until they are crisp and golden.

VEGETABLE AND PASTA SOUP

Preparation time: 20 minutes
Total cooking time: 40 minutes
Serves 6

2 teaspoons olive oil
1 onion, chopped
1 carrot, chopped
2 celery stalks, chopped
350 g (11 oz) sweet potato, chopped
400 g (13 oz) can corn kernels, drained
1 litre vegetable stock
1 cup (90 g/3 oz) pasta spirals

1 Heat the oil in a large pan and add the onion, carrot and celery. Cook over low heat, stirring regularly, for 10 minutes, or until soft.
2 Add the sweet potato, corn kernels and stock. Bring to the boil, reduce the heat and simmer for 20 minutes, or until the vegetables are tender.
3 Add the pasta to the pan and return to the boil. Reduce the heat and simmer for 10 minutes, or until the pasta is *al dente*. Serve immediately.

NUTRITION PER SERVE
Protein 4 g; Fat 2 g; Carbohydrate 25 g; Dietary Fibre 5 g; Cholesterol 0 mg; 555 kJ (135 cal)

Stir the onion, carrot and celery over low heat until soft.

Add the sweet potato, drained corn kernels and the stock.

When the vegetables are tender, add the pasta to the pan.

GREEK OCTOPUS IN RED WINE STEW

Preparation time: 25 minutes
Total cooking time:
1 hour 10 minutes
Serves 4–6

1 kg (2 lb) baby octopus
2 tablespoons olive oil
1 large onion, chopped
3 cloves garlic, crushed
1 bay leaf
3 cups (750 ml/24 fl oz) red wine
1/4 cup (60 ml/2 fl oz) red wine vinegar
400 g (13 oz) can crushed tomatoes
1 tablespoon tomato paste
1 tablespoon chopped fresh oregano
1/4 teaspoon ground cinnamon
small pinch ground cloves
1 teaspoon sugar
2 tablespoons finely chopped fresh flat-leaf parsley

1 Cut between the head and tentacles of the octopus, just below the eyes. Grasp the body and push the beak out and up through the centre of the tentacles with your fingers. Cut the eyes from the head by slicing a small round off. Discard the eye section. Carefully slit through one side, avoiding the ink sac, and remove any gut from inside. Rinse the octopus well under running water.

2 Heat the oil in a large saucepan, add the onion and cook over medium heat for 5 minutes, or until starting to brown. Add the garlic and bay leaf, and cook for 1 minute further. Add the octopus and stir to coat in the onion mixture.

3 Stir in the wine, vinegar, tomato, tomato paste, oregano, cinnamon, cloves and sugar. Bring to the boil, then reduce the heat and simmer for 1 hour, or until the octopus is tender and the sauce has thickened slightly. Stir in the parsley and season to taste with salt and pepper. Serve with a Greek salad and crusty bread.

NUTRITION PER SERVE (6)
Protein 29 g; Fat 8.5 g; Carbohydrate 3.5 g; Dietary Fibre 1.5 g; Cholesterol 332 mg; 1234 kJ (295 Cal)

Cut between the head and the tentacles of the octopus.

Slit the head section and remove any gut from the inside.

Add the octopus to the pan and stir to coat in the onion mixture.

Simmer until the octopus is tender and the sauce has thickened slightly.

CHICKEN AND COUSCOUS SOUP

Preparation time: 25 minutes
Total cooking time: 30 minutes
Serves 6

1 tablespoon olive oil
1 onion, sliced
1/2 teaspoon ground cumin
1/2 teaspoon paprika
1 teaspoon grated fresh ginger
1 clove garlic, crushed
2 celery sticks, sliced
2 small carrots, sliced
2 zucchini, sliced
1.125 litres chicken stock
2 chicken breast fillets, sliced
pinch saffron threads, optional
1/2 cup (95 g/3 oz) instant couscous
2 tablespoons chopped fresh parsley

1 Heat the oil in a large heavy-based pan. Add the onion and cook over medium heat for 10 minutes, or until very soft, stirring occasionally. Add the cumin, paprika, ginger and garlic and cook, stirring, for 1 minute further.
2 Add the celery, carrot and zucchini and stir to coat with the spices. Stir in the stock. Bring to the boil, then reduce the heat and simmer, partially covered, for about 15 minutes, or until the vegetables are tender.
3 Add the chicken and saffron to the pan and cook for about 5 minutes, or until the chicken is just tender; do not overcook. Stir in the couscous and chopped parsley and serve.

NUTRITION PER SERVE
Protein 19 g; Fat 5.5 g; Carbohydrate 12 g; Dietary Fibre 2 g; Cholesterol 37 mg; 712 kJ (170 cal)

HINT: Add the couscous to the soup just before serving because it absorbs liquid quickly and becomes very thick.

Add the spices to the pan with the onion and stir to thoroughly combine.

Stir the chicken stock into the vegetable and spice mixture.

Stir the chicken and saffron threads into the soup mixture.

Do not stir in the parsley and couscous until just before the soup is served.

SAFFRON CHICKEN

Preparation time: 25 minutes
Total cooking time: 1 hour 20 minutes
Serves 6

- 1 teaspoon saffron threads
- 2 tablespoons hot water
- 2 tablespoons oil
- 2 onions, chopped
- 3 cloves garlic, crushed
- 3 cm (1 1/4 inch) piece ginger, chopped
- 2 red chillies, seeded and sliced
- 1 teaspoon ground cardamom
- 1 teaspoon ground cumin
- 1/2 teaspoon ground turmeric
- 2 kg (4 lb) chicken pieces
- 2 cups (500 ml/16 fl oz) chicken stock

1 Fry the saffron threads in a dry frying pan over low heat for 1–2 minutes. Transfer to a small bowl, add the hot water and set aside.
2 Heat the oil in a pan over medium heat. Add the onion, garlic, ginger and chilli. Cover and cook for 10 minutes, or until very soft.
3 Add the cardamom, cumin and turmeric, and cook over medium heat for 2 minutes. Add the chicken pieces and cook over high heat for 3 minutes, or until the meat is well coated. Add the saffron liquid and the chicken stock. Bring to the boil, then reduce the heat and cook, covered, stirring occasionally, for 30 minutes.
4 Uncover, and cook for a further 20 minutes. Remove the chicken and keep warm. Reduce the stock to about 1 1/2 cups (375 ml/12 fl oz) over very high heat. Pour over the chicken. Season with salt and pepper, to taste.

NUTRITION PER SERVE
Protein 45 g; Fat 15 g; Carbohydrate 3 g; Dietary Fibre 1 g; Cholesterol 155 mg; 1445 kJ (345 cal)

Fry the saffron threads in a dry pan over low heat for 1–2 minutes.

Add the chopped onion, garlic, ginger and chilli and stir to combine.

Add the saffron threads with their liquid, and the stock to the pan.

Remove the chicken from the pan and reduce the stock over high heat.

LEMON CHICKEN SOUP

Preparation time: 10 minutes
Total cooking time: 10 minutes
Serves 4

2 chicken breast fillets
1 lemon
1 litre chicken stock (see Hint)
2 fresh lemon thyme sprigs, plus extra, to serve (see Note)

1 Trim any excess fat from the chicken. Using a vegetable peeler, cut 2 strips of rind from the lemon and remove the pith. Place the stock, rind and lemon thyme in a shallow pan and slowly bring almost to the boil. Reduce to simmering point, add the chicken and cook, covered, for 7 minutes, or until the meat is tender.
2 Remove the chicken from the pan, transfer to a plate and cover with foil.
3 Strain the stock into a clean pan through a sieve lined with 2 layers of damp muslin. Finely shred the chicken and return to the soup. Reheat gently and season to taste with salt and freshly ground black pepper. Serve immediately, garnished with the extra sprigs of lemon thyme.

NUTRITION PER SERVE
Protein 25 g; Fat 3 g; Carbohydrate 0 g; Dietary Fibre 0 g; Cholesterol 55 mg; 535 kJ (130 cal)

NOTE: You can use ordinary thyme if lemon thyme is not available.

HINT: If you don't have time to make your own stock, poultry shops or butchers sometimes sell their own. These may have more flavour and contain less salt than stock cubes.

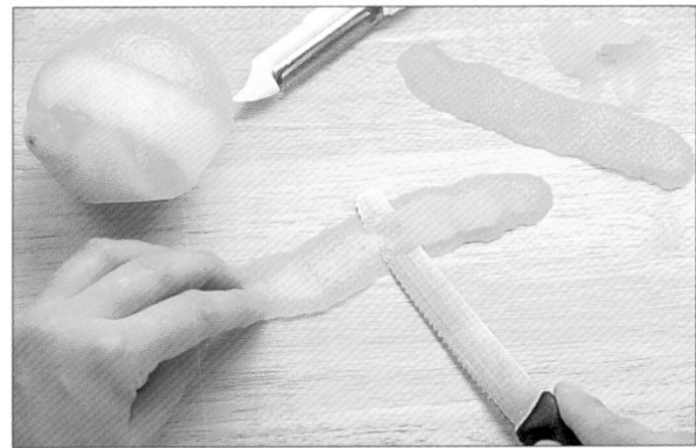

Using a small knife, remove the white pith from the lemon rind.

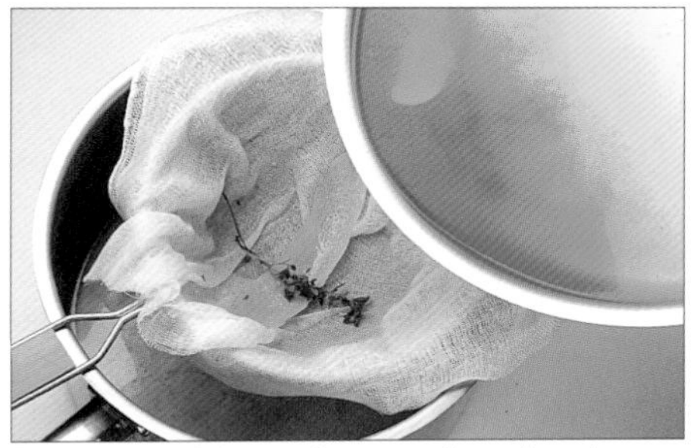

Pour the stock into a clean pan through a sieve lined with damp muslin.

Finely shred the chicken into thin pieces and return to the soup.

stir-fries

CHICKEN AND ASPARAGUS STIR-FRY

Preparation time: 15 minutes
Total cooking time: 10 minutes
Serves 4

- 2 tablespoons oil
- 1 clove garlic, crushed
- 10 cm (4 inch) piece fresh ginger, peeled and thinly sliced
- 3 chicken breast fillets, sliced
- 4 spring onions, sliced
- 200 g (6 1/2 oz) fresh asparagus spears, cut into short lengths
- 2 tablespoons soy sauce
- 1/3 cup (30 g/1 oz) slivered almonds, roasted

1 Heat a wok over high heat, add the oil and swirl to coat the side. Add the garlic, ginger and chicken and stir-fry for 1–2 minutes, or until the chicken changes colour.

2 Add the spring onion and asparagus and stir-fry for a further 2 minutes, or until the spring onion is soft.

3 Stir in the soy sauce and 1/4 cup (60 ml/2 fl oz) water, cover and simmer for 2 minutes, or until the chicken is tender and the vegetables are slightly crisp. Sprinkle with the almonds and serve immediately.

NUTRITION PER SERVE
Protein 30 g; Fat 12 g; Carbohydrate 2 g; Dietary Fibre 1 g; Cholesterol 60 mg; 1010 kJ (240 cal)

Stir-fry the garlic, ginger and chicken until the chicken changes colour.

Add the spring onion and asparagus and stir-fry until the spring onion is soft.

Stir in the soy sauce and a little water and cover the wok to steam the vegetables.

BLACK BEAN PORK WITH BOK CHOY

Preparation time: 20 minutes
Total cooking time: 10 minutes
Serves 4

- 400 g (13 oz) lean pork leg steaks
- 1 tablespoon canned salted black beans, rinsed
- 500 g (1 lb) baby bok choy
- 2 teaspoons sesame oil
- 2 onions, finely sliced
- 2 cloves garlic, finely chopped
- 2–3 teaspoons chopped ginger
- 1 red capsicum, cut into strips
- 1/2 cup (90 g/3 oz) water chestnuts, finely sliced
- 2 tablespoons oyster sauce
- 1 tablespoon soy sauce
- 2 teaspoons fish sauce

1 Slice the pork steaks into strips, cutting across the grain. Roughly chop the beans. Separate the leaves of the bok choy, trim away the tough ends and shred the leaves.

2 Heat half the sesame oil in a large wok. Cook the onion, garlic and ginger over high heat for 3–4 minutes, add the capsicum and cook for 2–3 minutes. Remove from the wok. Heat the remaining sesame oil and stir-fry the pork in batches over high heat.

3 Return all the pork to the wok along with the onion mixture, black beans, shredded bok choy, water chestnuts and oyster, soy and fish sauces. Toss quickly to combine the ingredients, lower the heat, cover and steam for 3–4 minutes, or until the bok choy has just wilted. Serve immediately.

NUTRITION PER SERVE
Protein 30 g; Fat 3 g; Carbohydrate 20 g; Dietary Fibre 3.5 g; Cholesterol 55 mg; 910 kJ (215 cal)

Separate the leaves of the bok choy and then trim the tough ends.

Stir-fry the pork strips in batches over high heat until brown.

Toss all the ingredients quickly until combined, then lower the heat.

FISH WITH GINGER

Preparation time: 20 minutes
Total cooking time: 15 minutes
Serves 4

1 tablespoon peanut oil
1 small onion, finely sliced
3 teaspoons ground coriander
600 g ($1\frac{1}{4}$ lb) boneless white fish fillets, such as perch, sliced
1 tablespoon julienned fresh ginger
1 teaspoon finely chopped and seeded green chilli
2 tablespoons lime juice
2 tablespoons coriander leaves

1 Heat a wok until very hot, add the oil and swirl to coat. Add the onion and stir-fry for 4 minutes, or until soft and golden. Add the ground coriander and cook for 1–2 minutes, or until the mixture is fragrant.

2 Add the fish, ginger and chilli, and stir-fry for 5–7 minutes, or until the fish is cooked through. Stir in the lime juice and season. Garnish with the coriander leaves and serve.

NUTRITION PER SERVE
Protein 30 g; Fat 9 g; Carbohydrate 1 g; Dietary Fibre 0.4 g; Cholesterol 105 mg; 895 kJ (214 cal)

Peel the fresh ginger and then cut the flesh into julienne strips.

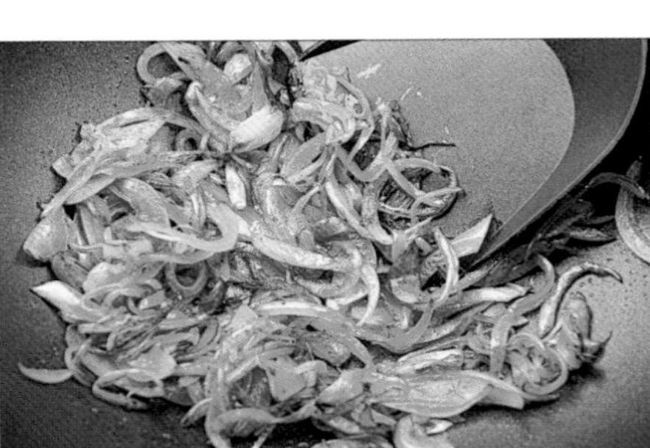

Stir-fry the onion for 4 minutes, or until it is soft and golden.

Add the fish, ginger and chilli to the wok and stir-fry until the fish is cooked through.

HONEY-BRAISED VEGETABLES WITH BEAN CURD

Preparation time: 30 minutes
+ 30 minutes soaking
Cooking time: 20 minutes
Serves 6

8 dried Chinese mushrooms
20 dried lily buds (see NOTE)
2 tablespoons peanut oil
3 thin slices fresh ginger, cut into strips
250 g (8 oz) white sweet potato, halved and sliced
2 tablespoons soy sauce
1 tablespoon honey
2 teaspoons sesame oil
60 g (2 oz) deep-fried tofu puffs, cut into thin strips
2 teaspoons cornflour
4 spring onions, cut into short lengths
410 g (13 oz) can baby corn
230 g ($7\frac{1}{2}$ oz) can water chestnuts, drained

1 Soak the mushrooms in hot water for 30 minutes. Drain, reserving $\frac{3}{4}$ cup (185 ml/6 fl oz) of the liquid. Squeeze dry with your hands. Remove the stems and slice the mushrooms thinly. Soak the lily buds separately in warm water for 30 minutes, then drain.
2 Heat the oil in a wok. Add the ginger and stir-fry for 1 minute. Add the mushrooms and lily buds and stir-fry for 30 seconds. Add the sweet potato with the soy, honey, sesame oil, mushroom liquid and tofu. Simmer in the wok for 15 minutes.
3 Dissolve the cornflour in a little water and add to the wok. Stir until the liquid thickens. Add the spring onions, corn and water chestnuts and toss to heat through before serving.

NUTRITION PER SERVE
Protein 4 g; Fat 10 g; Carbohydrate 30 g; Dietary Fibre 5 g; Cholesterol 0 mg; 920 kJ (220 cal)

NOTE: Dried lily buds are a Chinese speciality (see glossary of ingredients, pages 8–13). They can be left out without altering the flavour greatly.

Cut three thin slices of fresh ginger and then cut the slices into thin strips.

Add the sweet potato, soy, honey, sesame oil, mushroom liquid and tofu to the wok.

Stir until the sauce thickens, then add the spring onions, corn and water chestnuts.

PEPPERED CHICKEN

Preparation time: 10 minutes
Total cooking time: 10 minutes
Serves 4

1 tablespoon oil
2 chicken breast fillets, cut into strips
2 1/2 teaspoons seasoned peppercorns (see NOTE)
1 onion, cut into wedges
1 red capsicum, cut into strips
2 tablespoons oyster sauce
1 teaspoon soy sauce
1 teaspoon sugar

1 Heat a wok over high heat, add the oil and swirl to coat the base and side of the wok. Add the chicken strips and stir-fry for 2–3 minutes, or until they are browned.
2 Add the peppercorns and stir-fry until they are fragrant. Add the onion and capsicum and stir-fry for 2 minutes, or until the vegetables have softened slightly.
3 Reduce the heat and stir in the oyster sauce, soy and sugar. Toss well to thoroughly combine before serving.

NUTRITION PER SERVE
Protein 18 g; Fat 6.5 g; Carbohydrate 6 g; Dietary Fibre 1 g; Cholesterol 40 mg; 665 kJ (160 cal)

NOTE: Seasoned peppercorns are available in the herb and spice section of large supermarkets.

Add the strips of chicken breast to the wok and stir-fry until browned.

Add the onion and capsicum and stir-fry until they have softened slightly.

Add the oyster sauce, soy sauce and sugar to the stir-fry and toss through.

CHINESE BEEF AND SNOW PEAS

Preparation time: 10 minutes
Total cooking time: 5 minutes
Serves 4

400 g (13 oz) rump steak, finely sliced (see HINT)
2 tablespoons soy sauce
1/2 teaspoon grated fresh ginger
oil, for cooking
200 g (6 1/2 oz) snow peas, trimmed
1 1/2 teaspoons cornflour
1/2 cup (125 ml/4 fl oz) beef stock
1 teaspoon soy sauce, extra
1/4 teaspoon sesame oil

1 Put the meat in a glass or ceramic bowl. Mix the soy and ginger and add to the meat. Stir well. Heat the wok until very hot, add 2 tablespoons of the oil and swirl it around to coat the side. Add the beef and snow peas and stir-fry over high heat for 2 minutes, or until the meat changes colour.

2 Dissolve the cornflour in a little of the stock. Add to the wok with the remaining stock, extra soy and oil.

3 Stir until the sauce boils and thickens. Serve immediately.

NUTRITION PER SERVE
Protein 27 g; Fat 13 g; Carbohydrate 9 g; Dietary Fibre 3 g; Cholesterol 67 mg; 1088 kJ (260 cal)

HINT: To make the beef easier to slice, freeze it until it is just firm and thinly slice while it is still frozen.

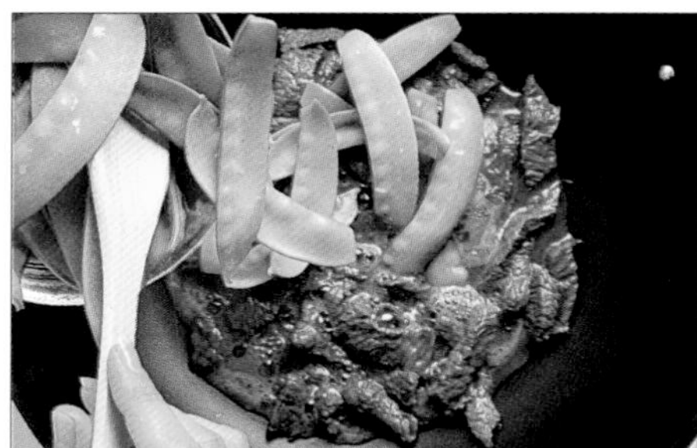

Stir-fry the beef and snow peas over high heat until the meat browns.

Dissolve the cornflour in a little of the stock and add to the wok with the rest of the stock.

Stir the beef and snow peas until the sauce comes to the boil and thickens.

GARLIC AND GINGER PRAWNS

Preparation time: 25 minutes
Total cooking time: 10 minutes
Serves 4

2 tablespoons oil
1 kg (2 lb) raw king prawns, peeled, deveined and butterflied, tails left intact
3–4 cloves garlic, finely chopped
5 cm (2 inch) piece fresh ginger, cut into matchsticks
2–3 small red chillies, seeded and finely chopped
6 coriander roots, finely chopped, plus a few leaves to garnish
8 spring onions, cut into short lengths
1/2 red capsicum, thinly sliced
2 tablespoons lemon juice
1/2 cup (125 ml/4 fl oz) white wine
2 teaspoons crushed palm sugar
2 teaspoons fish sauce

1 Heat the wok until very hot, add the oil and swirl to coat. Stir-fry the prawns, garlic, ginger, chilli and coriander root in two batches for 1–2 minutes over high heat, or until the prawns turn pink. Remove all the prawns from the wok and set aside.
2 Add the spring onion and capsicum to the wok. Cook over high heat for 2–3 minutes. Add the lemon juice, wine and palm sugar. Cook until the liquid has reduced by two thirds.
3 Add the prawns and sprinkle with fish sauce. Toss to heat through. Garnish with coriander to serve.

NUTRITION PER SERVE
Protein 1 g; Fat 10 g; Carbohydrate 4.5 g; Dietary Fibre 1.5 g; Cholesterol 0 mg; 550 kJ (130 cal)

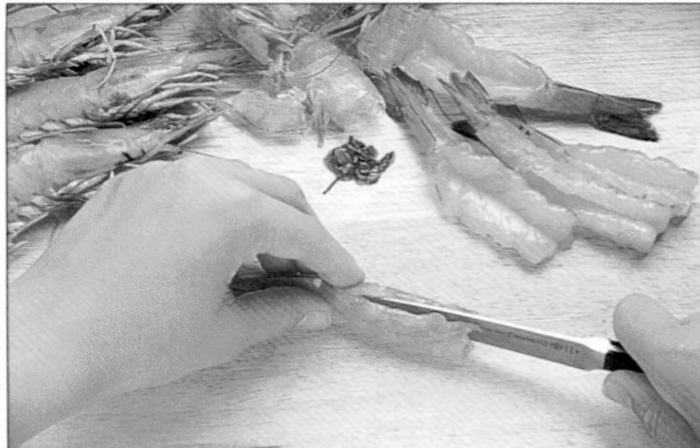

Butterfly the peeled prawns by cutting a slit down the backs and opening them out.

Using a large, sharp knife, finely chop the coriander roots.

Stir-fry the prawns in two batches with the garlic, ginger, chilli and coriander root.

STIR-FRIED EGGPLANT WITH LEMON

Preparation time: 20 minutes
+ 30 minutes standing
Total cooking time: 12 minutes
Serves 4

1 kg (2 lb) small eggplants
1 tablespoon salt
olive oil, for cooking
8 spring onions, sliced
3 cloves garlic, crushed
2 teaspoons cumin seeds
1 tablespoon ground coriander
1 teaspoon grated lemon rind
1/3 cup (80 ml/2 3/4 fl oz) lemon juice
2 teaspoons soft brown sugar
2 tablespoons coriander leaves

1 Peel the eggplants and cut into small cubes. Put in a colander and sprinkle with the salt. Leave for 30 minutes, then rinse under cold water and pat dry with paper towels.

2 Heat the wok until very hot, add 1 1/2 tablespoons of the oil and swirl it around to coat the side. Stir-fry the eggplant in two batches over high heat for 3–4 minutes, or until browned and cooked (use 1 1/2 tablespoons oil for each batch). Remove from the wok.

3 Return all the eggplant to the wok and add the spring onion. Stir-fry for 1 minute, or until the eggplant is soft. Add the garlic and cumin seeds, and cook for 1 minute. Stir in the ground coriander and cook for 30 seconds. Add the lemon rind, juice and sugar, and toss well. Season with salt and black pepper and sprinkle with coriander leaves before serving.

NUTRITION PER SERVE
Protein 3.5 g; Fat 10 g; Carbohydrate 10 g; Dietary Fibre 7 g; Cholesterol 0 mg; 640 kJ (155 cal)

Grate the lemon rind on the fine side of a metal grater, avoiding the bitter pith underneath.

Put the eggplant cubes in a colander and sprinkle with the salt to draw out any bitter juices.

Stir-fry the eggplant in batches until it is browned and cooked through.

SPICY PORK AND PRAWN LETTUCE PARCELS

Preparation time: 20 minutes
+ 30 minutes for lettuce crisping
Total cooking time: 10 minutes
Serves 4–6

1–2 large lettuces
1 tablespoon oil
3 spring onions, chopped
2 teaspoons red curry paste
100 g ($3^1/_2$ oz) pork mince
100 g ($3^1/_2$ oz) small raw prawns, peeled and deveined
3 tablespoons coconut milk
1–2 teaspoons chopped red chillies
2 teaspoons fish sauce
1 teaspoon soft brown sugar
2 teaspoons grated lime rind
3 tablespoons finely chopped roasted unsalted peanuts

1 Separate the lettuce leaves, wash them and pat dry, then wrap in a dry tea towel and refrigerate for about 30 minutes to crisp up.
2 Heat the oil in a wok. Add the spring onions and curry paste and stir-fry for 2 minutes over medium heat.
3 Add the pork mince and stir-fry until browned. Add the prawns, coconut milk and chillies and stir-fry for 3 minutes.
4 Add the fish sauce, brown sugar and lime rind and stir well. Stir in the peanuts, then leave to cool for 15 minutes. Place a spoonful of spicy pork on each lettuce leaf—the parcels can be rolled for easy eating.

NUTRITION PER SERVE (6)
Protein 10 g; Fat 8.5 g; Carbohydrate 3 g; Dietary Fibre 2 g; Cholesterol 33 mg; 535 kJ (128 cal)

NOTE: The filling must be cooled so that all liquid will be absorbed, making it moist and succulent.

Separate the lettuce leaves, wash and pat dry, then wrap in a tea towel and refrigerate.

Use a wooden spoon to stir the spring onions and curry paste in the wok.

Add the prawns, coconut milk and chillies to the wok and stir for 3 minutes.

Finally, add the chopped peanuts and stir through the mixture.

BABY OCTOPUS WITH GINGER AND LIME

Preparation time: 30 minutes
+ overnight marinating
Total cooking time: 10 minutes
Serves 4

500 g (1 lb) baby octopus
1/4 cup (15 g/1/2 oz) chopped coriander
2 cloves garlic, finely chopped
2 red chillies, seeded and chopped
2 teaspoons grated fresh ginger
2 stems lemon grass, white part only, chopped
1 tablespoon oil
2 tablespoons lime juice
oil, for cooking
550 g (1 lb 2 oz) bok choy, leaves separated
400 g (13 oz) choy sum, leaves separated
2 cloves garlic, crushed, extra
1 teaspoon grated fresh ginger, extra

1 To prepare the baby octopus, remove the head, cut off the eyes, and remove the gut by slitting the head open. Grasp the body firmly and push the beak out with your index finger. Clean the octopus thoroughly under cold running water and pat dry with paper towels. Cut the head into two or three pieces.
2 Place the octopus, coriander, garlic, chilli, ginger, lemon grass, oil and lime juice in a glass bowl. Cover and refrigerate overnight, or for 2 hours.
3 Heat the wok until very hot, add 1 tablespoon of the oil and swirl it around to coat the side. Stir-fry the vegetables with 1 tablespoon water. Cover and steam until just wilted. Spread on a serving plate.
4 Reheat the wok, add 1 tablespoon of the oil and stir-fry the extra garlic and ginger for 30 seconds, or until fragrant. Add the octopus and stir-fry over high heat for 7–8 minutes, or until cooked through. Serve on top of the wilted greens.

NUTRITION PER SERVE
Protein 25 g; Fat 6 g; Carbohydrate 8 g; Dietary Fibre 2 g; Cholesterol 0 mg; 735 kJ (175 cal)

Remove the eyes from the octopus by cutting them off the base of the head.

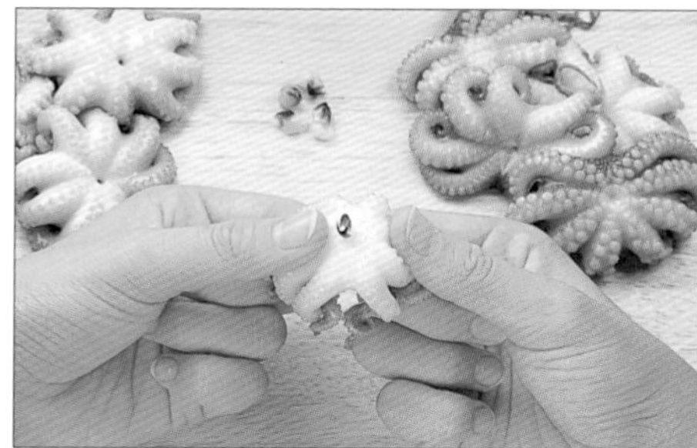

Remove and discard the beak by pushing it out of the octopus.

GINGER CHICKEN WITH BLACK FUNGUS

Preparation time: 25 minutes
Total cooking time: 15 minutes
Serves 4

- 3 tablespoons black fungus (see NOTE)
- 1 tablespoon oil
- 3 cloves garlic, chopped
- 5 cm (2 inches) ginger, shredded
- 500 g (1 lb) chicken breast fillets, sliced
- 4 spring onions, chopped
- 1 tablespoon Golden Mountain sauce
- 1 tablespoon fish sauce
- 2 teaspoons brown sugar
- 1/2 red capsicum, finely sliced
- 1/2 cup (15 g/1/2 oz) coriander leaves
- 1/2 cup (30 g/1 oz) shredded Thai basil leaves

1 Place the fungus in a bowl of hot water for 15 minutes until it is soft and swollen; drain and chop roughly.
2 Heat the oil in a large wok and stir-fry the garlic and ginger for 1 minute. Add the chicken in batches, stir-frying over high heat until it is cooked. Return all the chicken to the wok. Add the onions and Golden Mountain sauce and cook for 1 minute.
3 Add the fish sauce, brown sugar and fungus to the wok. Toss well, cover and steam for 2 minutes. Serve immediately, scattered with red capsicum, coriander and basil.

NUTRITION PER SERVE
Protein 6 g; Fat 5 g; Carbohydrate 4.5 g; Dietary Fibre 1 g; Cholesterol 8.5 mg; 359 kJ (86 cal)

NOTE: Black fungus is a dried mushroom that swells to many times its size when soaked in hot water. It is available from Asian food speciality stores and is also known as 'wood ear' or 'cloud ear' mushroom.

When the fungus is soft and swollen, drain it well and chop it with a sharp knife.

Add the spring onions and Golden Mountain sauce and stir-fry for a minute.

Cover the wok and allow the stir-fry to steam for 2 minutes.

CORIANDER PORK WITH FRESH PINEAPPLE

Preparation time: 25 minutes
Total cooking time: 10–12 minutes
Serves 4

400 g (13 oz) pork loin or fillet
1/4 pineapple
1 tablespoon oil
4 cloves garlic, chopped
4 spring onions, chopped
1 tablespoon fish sauce
1 tablespoon lime juice
1/2 cup (15 g/1/2 oz) coriander leaves
3 tablespoons chopped mint

1 Cut the pork into thin slices, using a very sharp knife (see HINT).
2 Trim the skin from the pineapple and cut the flesh into small bite-sized pieces. Heat the oil in a wok, add the garlic and spring onion and cook for 1 minute. Remove from the wok.
3 Heat the wok to very hot; add the pork in 2 or 3 batches and stir-fry each batch for 3 minutes or until the meat is just cooked. Return the meat, garlic and spring onion to the wok and then add the pineapple pieces, fish sauce and lime juice. Toss well. Just before serving, sprinkle with the coriander leaves and chopped mint and then toss together lightly.

NUTRITION PER SERVE
Protein 24 g; Fat 7 g; Carbohydrate 7 g; Dietary Fibre 2 g; Cholesterol 50 mg; 762 kJ (182 cal)

HINT: To make the meat easier to slice, freeze it until it is just firm and slice thinly while still frozen.

Buy pork loin or fillet and use a sharp knife to cut it into thin slices.

Slice the skin from the pineapple and cut the flesh into small, bite-sized pieces.

Stir-fry each batch of pork for 3 minutes, or until just cooked.

BEEF WITH OYSTER SAUCE

Preparation time: 15 minutes
Total cooking time: 5 minutes
Serves 4

1 1/2 teaspoons cornflour
1/2 cup (125 ml/4 fl oz) beef stock
2 tablespoons oyster sauce
1 teaspoon finely crushed garlic
1 teaspoon caster sugar
oil, for cooking
350 g (12 oz) rump steak, finely sliced
250 g (8 oz) beans, topped and tailed, cut into 5 cm (2 inch) lengths
1 small red capsicum, sliced
1/2 cup (60 g/2 oz) bean sprouts

1 Dissolve the cornflour in a little of the stock. Mix with the remaining stock, oyster sauce, garlic and sugar and set aside.

2 Heat the wok until very hot, add 1 tablespoon of the oil and swirl it around to coat the side. Add the beef in batches and stir-fry over high heat for 2 minutes, or until it browns.

3 Add the beans and capsicum and stir-fry another minute.

4 Add the cornflour mixture to the wok and cook until the sauce boils and thickens. Stir in the bean sprouts and serve immediately.

NUTRITION PER SERVE

Protein 23 g; Fat 12 g; Carbohydrate 10 g; Dietary Fibre 2.5 g; Cholesterol 60 mg; 1016 kJ (243 cal)

Brown the steak in batches so the wok doesn't overcrowd and reduce the temperature.

Add the beans and capsicum to the browned meat and stir-fry for 1 minute.

Add the mixture of stock and cornflour and stir until the sauce boils and thickens.

SMOKED CHICKEN AND SPINACH

Preparation time: 10 minutes
Total cooking time: 10 minutes
Serves 4

300 g (10 oz) smoked chicken breast (see NOTE)
1 tablespoon olive oil
100 g (3 1/2 oz) marinated chargrilled capsicum, cut into thin strips
1/3 cup (50 g/1 3/4 oz) pine nuts
1 bunch (500 g/1 lb) English spinach, trimmed
1 tablespoon light sour cream
2 teaspoons wholegrain mustard
1/4 cup (7 g/1/4 oz) basil leaves, finely shredded

1 Cut the chicken into thin strips.
2 Heat a wok over high heat, add the oil and swirl to coat the base and side of the wok with oil. Add the chicken, capsicum and pine nuts and stir-fry for 3–4 minutes, or until the nuts are golden. Add the spinach and stir-fry for 2–3 minutes, or until wilted.
3 Add the sour cream, mustard and basil to the wok and toss well to thoroughly combine. Season with salt and pepper before serving.

NUTRITION PER SERVE
Protein 22 g; Fat 13 g; Carbohydrate 2.5 g; Dietary Fibre 4.5 g; Cholesterol 45 mg; 900 kJ (215 cal)

NOTE: Smoked chicken breast and marinated chargrilled capsicum are available at speciality delicatessens.

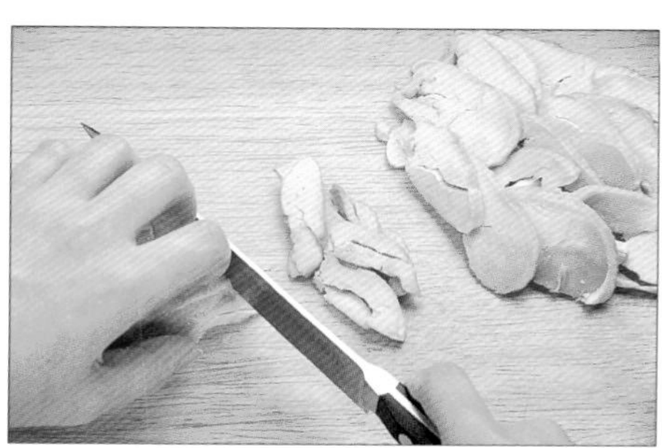

Cut the smoked chicken breast into thin strips for quick and even stir-frying.

Stir-fry the chicken, capsicum and pine nuts until the nuts are golden.

Add the sour cream, mustard and basil to the stir-fry and toss through.

PORK WITH SNAKE BEANS

Preparation time: 15 minutes
Total cooking time: 20 minutes
Serves 4

oil, for cooking
400 g (13 oz) pork fillet, cut into thick slices
2 onions, thinly sliced
150 g (5 oz) snake beans, diagonally sliced (see NOTE)
3 cloves garlic, finely chopped
1 tablespoon finely chopped fresh ginger
1 red capsicum, thinly sliced
6 spring onions, diagonally sliced
2 tablespoons sweet chilli sauce

1 Heat the wok until very hot, add 2 teaspoons of the oil and swirl it around to coat the side. Stir-fry the pork in two batches over high heat for 3–4 minutes, or until it is just cooked, adding more oil when necessary. Remove all the pork from the wok.

2 Heat 1 tablespoon of the oil over medium heat and add the sliced onion. Cook for 3–4 minutes, or until the onion has softened slightly. Add the sliced snake beans and cook for 2–3 minutes. Add the garlic, ginger, capsicum and spring onion, and toss well. Increase the heat and cook for 3–4 minutes.

3 Return the pork to the wok, add the sweet chilli sauce and toss well. Remove from the heat and season with salt and pepper. Serve immediately.

NUTRITION PER SERVE
Protein 25 g; Fat 12 g; Carbohydrate 8 g; Dietary Fibre 4 g; Cholesterol 50 mg; 1005 kJ (240 cal)

NOTE: If you can't find snake beans you can use ordinary green beans in this recipe.

Top and tail the snake beans, then cut them into diagonal slices.

SWEET CHILLI SQUID

Preparation time: 20 minutes
Total cooking time: 10 minutes
Serves 4

- 750 g ($1\frac{1}{2}$ lb) squid tubes
- 1 tablespoon peanut oil
- 1 tablespoon finely grated fresh ginger
- 2 cloves garlic, crushed
- 8 spring onions, chopped
- 2 tablespoons sweet chilli sauce
- 2 tablespoons Chinese barbecue sauce
- 1 tablespoon soy sauce
- 550 g (1 lb 2 oz) bok choy, cut into short pieces
- 1 tablespoon chopped coriander leaves

1 Cut the squid tubes open, score diagonal slashes across the inside surface and cut into strips.
2 Heat a wok until very hot, add the oil and swirl to coat. Add the ginger, garlic, spring onion and squid and stir-fry for 3 minutes, or until browned.
3 Add the sauces and 2 tablespoons water to the wok and stir-fry for 2 minutes, or until the squid is just tender. Add the bok choy and coriander, and stir-fry for 1 minute, or until the bok choy is tender.

NUTRITION PER SERVE
Protein 40 g; Fat 8 g; Carbohydrate 4 g; Dietary Fibre 7.5 g; Cholesterol 375 mg; 1030 kJ (245 cal)

NOTE: Squid should be cooked at a very high temperature but quite quickly. If you cook it for too long it will toughen.

Rinse the bok choy thoroughly, then cut it into short pieces.

Score diagonal slashes across the inside surface of the squid tubes, then cut into strips.

Stir-fry the squid for 3 minutes. The score marks in the flesh will make it curl nicely.

QUICK THAI CHICKEN

Preparation time: 15 minutes
Total cooking time: 15 minutes
Serves 4

- 1 tablespoon red curry paste
- 2 tablespoons oil
- 2 tablespoons fish sauce
- 2 tablespoons lime juice
- 1/4 cup (15 g/1/2 oz) chopped coriander leaves
- 1 tablespoon grated fresh ginger
- 1 teaspoon caster sugar
- 1 teaspoon sesame oil
- 750 g (1 1/2 lb) chicken thigh fillets, cut into strips
- 1 tablespoon oil, extra
- 10 spring onions, cut into short lengths
- 100 g (3 1/2 oz) snow peas, trimmed

1 Whisk together the curry paste, oil, fish sauce, lime juice, coriander, ginger, sugar and sesame oil in a large non-metallic bowl. Add the chicken strips and toss to coat thoroughly.

2 Heat the extra oil in a wok. Add the chicken in batches and stir-fry for 3–5 minutes, or until browned all over, then remove from the wok and set aside. Add the spring onion and snow peas and stir-fry for 2 minutes. Return the chicken and any juices to the wok and stir-fry for 2–3 minutes, or until the chicken is heated through. Season with salt and pepper and serve.

NUTRITION PER SERVE
Protein 45 g; Fat 10 g; Carbohydrate 6 g; Dietary Fibre 2.5 g; Cholesterol 95 mg; 1275 kJ (305 cal)

Cut the chicken thigh fillets into strips, then marinate in the Thai sauce.

Brown the chicken in batches so that the wok doesn't overcrowd and cool down.

Stir-fry the spring onion and snow peas for a couple of minutes before adding the chicken.

FISH CUTLETS IN SPICY RED SAUCE

Preparation time: 10 minutes
Total cooking time: 35 minutes
Serves 4

- 1 tablespoon oil
- 2 onions, finely chopped
- 4 ripe tomatoes, peeled and chopped
- 1 tablespoon sambal oelek
- 1 tablespoon soft brown sugar
- 4 blue-eyed cod cutlets or other firm fish cutlets
- 2 tablespoons fish sauce
- 2 tablespoons rice vinegar or white vinegar
- 2 tablespoooons chopped coriander

1 Heat the oil in a wok or large frying pan and add the onion. Cook over medium heat for 2 minutes or until soft but not browned. Add the tomatoes, sambal oelek, brown sugar and 3 tablespoons of water. Bring to the boil, then reduce the heat, cover the wok and simmer for 20 minutes or until the sauce is thick.

2 Add the fish cutlets to the wok and spoon some sauce over them. Cover the wok and cook for 3–5 minutes. Turn the fish to cook the other side. (If the wok isn't big enough you can cook the fish in two batches.)

3 Remove the fish from the wok. Add the fish sauce, vinegar and chopped coriander to the sauce in the wok and stir well before spooning the sauce over the fish.

NUTRITION PER SERVE
Protein 20 g; Fat 7 g; Carbohydrate 9 g; Dietary Fibre 2 g; Cholesterol 55 mg; 734 kJ (175 cal)

Add the chopped tomatoes, sambal oelek, brown sugar and water to the wok.

Place the fish cutlets in the wok, in batches if necessary, and spoon some sauce over.

Transfer the fish to serving plates and add the fish sauce, vinegar and coriander to the wok.

SWEET AND SOUR PORK

Preparation time: 25 minutes
+ 30 minutes marinating
Total cooking time: 20 minutes
Serves 4

500 g (1 lb) pork fillet, cut into thick slices
2 tablespoons cornflour
1 tablespoon sherry
1 tablespoon soy sauce
1 tablespoon sugar
oil, for cooking
1 large onion, thinly sliced
1 green capsicum, cut into cubes
2 small carrots, thinly sliced
1 small Lebanese cucumber, seeded and chopped
5 spring onions, cut into short lengths
440 g (14 oz) can pineapple pieces in natural juice, drained, juice reserved
1/4 cup (60 ml/2 fl oz) white vinegar
1/2 teaspoon salt

1 Place the pork in a shallow glass or ceramic bowl. Combine the cornflour with the sherry, soy sauce and half the sugar and pour into the bowl. Cover and refrigerate for 30 minutes.
2 Drain the pork, reserving the marinade. Heat the wok until very hot, add 2 tablespoons of the oil and swirl to coat the side. Stir-fry half the pork over high heat for 4–5 minutes, or until the pork is golden brown and just cooked. Remove from the wok, add more oil if necessary and repeat with the remaining pork. Remove all the pork from the wok.
3 Reheat the wok, add 1 tablespoon of the oil and stir-fry the onion over high heat for 3–4 minutes, or until slightly softened. Add the capsicum and carrot, and cook for 3–4 minutes, or until tender. Stir in the marinade, cucumber, spring onion, pineapple, vinegar, salt, remaining sugar and 4 tablespoons of the reserved pineapple juice.
4 Bring to the boil and simmer for 2–3 minutes, or until the sauce has thickened slightly. Return the pork to the wok and toss until the pork is heated through. Serve immediately.

NUTRITION PER SERVE
Protein 25 g; Fat 12 g; Carbohydrate 25 g; Dietary Fibre 4 g; Cholesterol 50 mg; 1325 kJ (315 cal)

Peel the carrots, if necessary, and cut them into thin diagonal slices.

Halve the cucumber lengthways and scoop out the seeds with a teaspoon.

Stir-fry the pork until it is golden brown and just cooked through.

VIETNAMESE PRAWNS WITH SNAKE BEANS

Preparation time: 25 minutes
Total cooking time: 15 minutes
Serves 4

2 tablespoons oil
2 onions, very finely sliced
5 cloves garlic, finely chopped
2 stems lemon grass, white part only, very finely sliced
3 red chillies, seeded and finely sliced
250 g (8 oz) snake beans, topped and tailed and cut into short pieces
300 g (10 oz) raw prawns, peeled and deveined
2 teaspoons sugar
1 tablespoon fish sauce
1 tablespoon rice wine vinegar
garlic chives, to garnish

1 Heat the oil in a large wok. Add the onion, garlic, lemon grass and chilli and stir-fry over medium-high heat for 4 minutes or until soft and golden.
2 Add the beans to the wok and stir-fry for 2–3 minutes or until bright green. Add the prawns and sugar and toss gently for 3 minutes.
3 Season with the fish sauce and rice wine vinegar, toss well and serve, sprinkled with garlic chives.

NUTRITION PER SERVE
Protein 18 g; Fat 10 g; Carbohydrate 4 g; Dietary Fibre 2.5 g; Cholesterol 112 mg; 765 kJ (183 cal)

NOTE: Snake beans are very long, dark green beans, about 30 cm (12 inches) long, with pointed tips. They are sold in bunches at speciality fruit and vegetable and Asian food stores. If they are not available, green beans can be used.

Top and tail the snake beans and then cut them into short pieces.

Stir-fry the onion, garlic, lemon grass and chilli in the wok.

Add the chopped snake beans to the wok and stir-fry until they are bright green.

CHICKEN SAN CHOY BAU

Preparation time: 10 minutes
Total cooking time: 5 minutes
Serves 4 as a starter

1 tablespoon oil
700 g (1 lb 6 oz) chicken mince
2 cloves garlic, finely chopped
100 g ($3^1/_2$ oz) can water chestnuts, drained, chopped
$1^1/_2$ tablespoons oyster sauce
3 teaspoons soy sauce
1 teaspoon sugar
5 spring onions, finely sliced
4 lettuce leaves

1 Heat a wok over high heat, add the oil and swirl to coat the base and side of the wok. Add the chicken mince and garlic and stir-fry for 3–4 minutes, or until browned and cooked through, breaking up any lumps with the back of a spoon. Pour off any excess liquid.
2 Reduce the heat and add the water chestnuts, oyster sauce, soy sauce, sugar and spring onion.
3 Trim the lettuce leaves around the edges to neaten them and to form each one into a cup shape. Divide the chicken mixture among the lettuce cups and serve hot, with extra oyster sauce if you like.

NUTRITION PER SERVE
Protein 40 g; Fat 9 g; Carbohydrate 6 g; Dietary Fibre 2 g; Cholesterol 88 mg; 1142 kJ (273 cal)

Stir-fry the chicken mince, breaking up any lumps with the back of a spoon.

Add the water chestnuts, oyster sauce, soy sauce, sugar and spring onion.

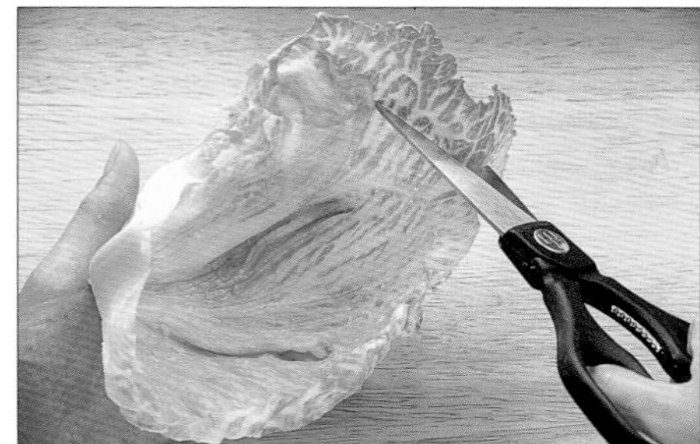

Trim the edges of the lettuce leaves and form them into cup shapes to hold the mince.

MUSSELS WITH LEMON GRASS, BASIL AND WINE

Preparation time: 30 minutes
Total cooking time: 15 minutes
Serves 4–6

1 kg (2 lb) black mussels
1 tablespoon oil
1 onion, chopped
4 cloves garlic, chopped
2 stems lemon grass,white part only, chopped
1–2 teaspoons chopped small red chillies
1 cup (250 ml/8 fl oz) white wine
1 tablespoon fish sauce
1 cup (30 g/1 oz) Thai basil leaves, roughly chopped

1 Scrub the mussels and debeard. Soak them in a bowl of cold water for 10 minutes; drain and discard any that are open and don't close when tapped on the work surface.
2 Heat the oil in a wok and stir-fry the onion, garlic, lemon grass and chilli over low heat for 4 minutes. Add the wine and fish sauce and cook for 3 minutes.
3 Add the mussels to the wok and toss well. Cover the wok; increase the heat and cook for 3–4 minutes or until the mussels open. Discard any that don't open. Add the chopped basil and toss well before serving.

NUTRITION PER SERVE (6)
Protein 13 g; Fat 5 g; Carbohydrate 1.5 g; Dietary Fibre 0 g; Cholesterol 30 mg; 1271 kJ (302 cal)

HINT: Do not overcook the mussels or they will become tough. Use small fresh black mussels and buy a few extra, in case any are cracked, damaged or already open.

After scrubbing the mussels with a brush, pull the beards off and discard.

Add the wine and fish sauce to the wok and cook for 3 minutes.

If any mussels have not opened during cooking, discard them.

LIME AND GARLIC PRAWNS WITH SUGAR SNAP PEAS

Preparation time: 10 minutes
Total cooking time: 3 minutes
Serves 4

$1/2$ cup (125 ml/4 fl oz) freshly squeezed lime juice
3 tablespoons soy sauce
$1\,1/2$ tablespoons honey
1 tablespoon peanut oil
2 cloves garlic, crushed
4 kaffir lime leaves, shredded
16 ears of baby corn, halved lengthways
150 g (5 oz) sugar snap peas
24 raw prawns, peeled and deveined, tails intact
4 tablespoons fresh coriander leaves, chopped

1 Place the lime juice, soy sauce and honey in a small bowl and stir until the honey dissolves.
2 Heat a wok over high heat, add the oil and swirl to coat the side. Add the garlic, lime leaves and baby corn and stir-fry for 1–2 minutes.
3 Add the sugar snap peas, prawns and lime juice mixture and stir-fry for a further minute, or until the prawns are cooked through. Stir in the coriander leaves and serve immediately.

NUTRITION PER SERVE
Protein 27 g; Fat 5.5 g; Carbohydrate 23 g; Dietary Fibre 5 g; Cholesterol 150 mg; 930 kJ (222 cal)

NOTE: To keep kaffir lime leaves fresh, keep them in an airtight container or plastic bag in the freezer. They will defrost within 1 minute.

Stir the lime juice, soy sauce and honey until the honey dissolves.

Add the sugar snap peas, prawns and lime juice mixture to the wok and stir-fry.

pan-fries & grills

STEAK IN RED WINE

Preparation time: 10 minutes + 3 hours marinating
Total cooking time: 10 minutes
Serves 4

750 g (1½ lb) rump steak
1 cup (250 ml/8 fl oz) good red wine
2 teaspoons garlic salt
1 tablespoon dried oregano leaves
cracked black pepper

1 Trim the steak of any fat. Mix together the wine, salt, oregano and pepper. Put the steak in a shallow, non-metallic dish and add the marinade. Toss well, cover and refrigerate for at least 3 hours.

2 Cook the steak on a hot, lightly oiled barbecue flatplate or grill for 3–4 minutes on each side, brushing frequently with the marinade.

NUTRITION PER SERVE
Protein 44 g; Fat 5 g; Carbohydrate 0 g; Dietary Fibre 0 g; Cholesterol 126 mg; 1100 kJ (264 cal)

Trim the steak of any excess fat and sinew before marinating.

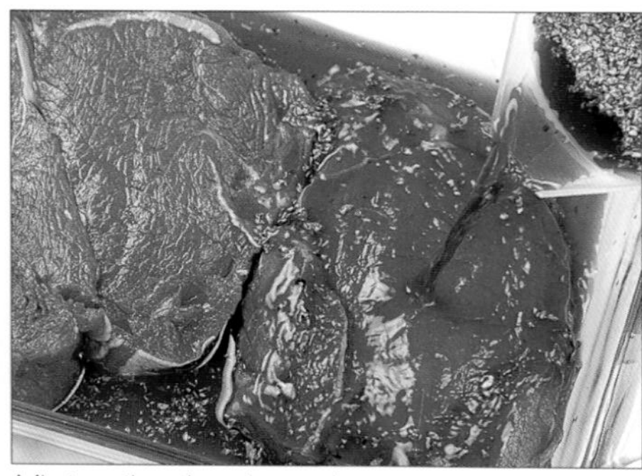

Mix together the wine, salt, oregano and pepper and pour over the steak.

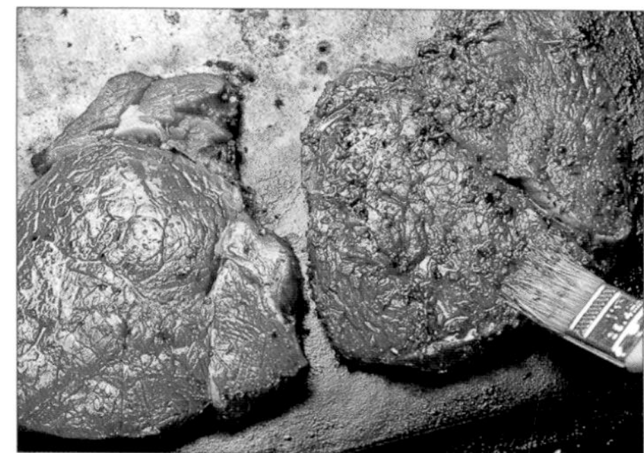

Cook the steak on a hot barbecue, brushing frequently with the wine marinade.

BLACKENED CAJUN SPICED CHICKEN

Preparation time: 15 minutes + 30 minutes standing
Total cooking time: 1 hour
Serves 4

1½ tablespoons onion powder
1½ tablespoons garlic powder
2 teaspoons paprika
1 teaspoon white pepper
2 teaspoons dried thyme
½–1 teaspoon chilli powder (see NOTE)
8 chicken drumsticks, scored

1 Combine the herbs, spices and 1 teaspoon salt in a plastic bag. Place the drumsticks in the bag and shake until all the pieces are coated. Leave the chicken in the fridge for at least 30 minutes to allow the flavours to develop, or overnight if time permits.
2 Cook the chicken on a lightly oiled barbecue grill for 55–60 minutes, or until slightly blackened and cooked through. Brush lightly with some oil to prevent drying out during cooking.

NUTRITION PER SERVE
Protein 25 g; Fat 7 g; Carbohydrate 0 g; Dietary Fibre 0 g; Cholesterol 103 mg; 660 kJ (160 cal)

NOTE: Chilli powder is very hot, so only use ½ teaspoon if you prefer a milder flavour.

Put the herbs, spices and salt in a freezer bag, add the chicken and shake to coat.

Cook the chicken for 55–60 minutes, or until slightly blackened.

LAMB CHOPS WITH CITRUS POCKETS

Preparation time: 25 minutes
Total cooking time: 15 minutes
Serves 4

4 lamb chump chops, about 250 g (8 oz) each
2 tablespoons lemon juice

CITRUS FILLING
3 spring onions, finely chopped
1 celery stick, finely chopped
2 teaspoons grated fresh ginger
3/4 cup (60 g/2 oz) fresh breadcrumbs
2 tablespoons orange juice
2 teaspoons finely grated orange rind
1 teaspoon chopped fresh rosemary

1 Cut a deep, long pocket in the side of each lamb chop.
2 Mix together all the filling ingredients and spoon into the pockets in the lamb.
3 Cook on a hot, lightly oiled barbecue flatplate or grill, turning once, for 15 minutes, or until the lamb is cooked through but still pink in the centre. Drizzle with the lemon juice.

NUTRITION PER SERVE
Protein 35 g; Fat 5 g; Carbohydrate 15 g; Dietary Fibre 1 g; Cholesterol 105 mg; 1080 kJ (335 cal)

Cut a deep, long pocket in the side of each lamb chop, right through the skin and fat.

Mix together all the filling ingredients and then spoon into the lamb pockets.

Cook the lamb chops on a hot barbecue flatplate, turning once.

VIETNAMESE FISH

Preparation time: 25 minutes + 20 minutes marinating
Total cooking time: 15 minutes
Serves 6

750 g (1 1/2 lb) small, firm, white fish
2 teaspoons green peppercorns, finely crushed
2 teaspoons chopped red chilli
3 teaspoons fish sauce
2 teaspoons oil
1 tablespoon oil, extra
2 onions, finely sliced
4 cm (1 1/2 inch) piece of fresh ginger, peeled and thinly sliced
3 cloves garlic, finely sliced
2 teaspoons sugar
4 spring onions, cut into short lengths, then finely shredded

LEMON AND GARLIC DIPPING SAUCE
3 tablespoons lemon juice
2 tablespoons fish sauce
1 tablespoon sugar
2 small red chillies, chopped
3 cloves garlic, crushed

1 Cut 2 diagonal slashes in the thickest part of the fish on both sides. In a food processor or mortar and pestle, grind the peppercorns, chilli and fish sauce to a paste and brush over the fish. Leave for 20 minutes.
2 Cook on a hot, lightly oiled barbecue grill or flatplate for 8 minutes on each side, or until the flesh flakes easily when tested.
3 While the fish is cooking, heat the extra oil in a pan and stir the onion over medium heat, until golden. Add the ginger, garlic and sugar and cook for 3 minutes. Place the fish on a serving plate, top with the onion mixture and sprinkle with spring onion.
4 To make the dipping sauce, mix together all the ingredients. Serve with the barbecued fish.

NUTRITION PER SERVE
Protein 27 g; Fat 5 g; Carbohydrate 3 g; Dietary Fibre 1 g; Cholesterol 88 mg; 705 kJ (168 cal)

Cut diagonal slashes into the thickest part of the fish so that it cooks through evenly.

Lightly brush the chilli mixture over the surface of the fish.

Cook the finely sliced onion over medium heat, stirring until golden.

CHARGRILLED CHICKEN

Preparation time: 20 minutes
+ 2 hours marinating
Total cooking time: 1 hour
Serves 4

4 chicken breast fillets
2 tablespoons honey
1 tablespoon wholegrain mustard
1 tablespoon soy sauce
2 red onions, cut into wedges
8 Roma tomatoes, halved lengthways
2 tablespoons soft brown sugar
2 tablespoons balsamic vinegar
cooking oil spray
snow pea sprouts, for serving

1 Preheat the oven to moderate 180°C (350°F/Gas 4). Trim the chicken of any excess fat and place in a shallow dish. Combine the honey, mustard and soy sauce and pour over the chicken, tossing to coat. Cover and refrigerate for 2 hours, turning once.

2 Place the onion wedges and tomato halves on a baking tray covered with baking paper. Sprinkle with the sugar and drizzle with the balsamic vinegar. Bake for 40 minutes.

3 Heat a chargrill pan or barbecue hotplate and lightly spray with oil. Remove the chicken from the marinade and cook for 4–5 minutes on each side, or until cooked through. Slice the chicken and serve with the snow pea sprouts, tomato halves and onion wedges.

NUTRITION PER SERVE

Protein 25 g; Fat 2.5 g; Carbohydrate 30 g; Dietary Fibre 3 g; Cholesterol 50 mg; 990 kJ (235 cal)

Pour the marinade over the chicken and toss to coat thoroughly.

Drizzle the balsamic vinegar over the onion wedges and tomato halves.

Cook the marinated chicken in a hot, lightly oiled chargrill pan.

BEEF STROGANOFF

Preparation time: 20 minutes
Total cooking time: 25 minutes
Serves 4

500 g (1 lb) rump steak
cooking oil spray
1 onion, sliced
1/4 teaspoon paprika
250 g (8 oz) button mushrooms, halved
2 tablespoons tomato paste
1/2 cup (125 ml/4 fl oz) beef stock
1/2 cup (125 ml/4 fl oz) low-fat evaporated milk
3 teaspoons cornflour
3 tablespoons chopped fresh parsley

1 Remove any excess fat from the steak and slice into thin strips. Cook in batches in a large, lightly greased non-stick frying pan over high heat, until just cooked. Remove from the pan.
2 Lightly spray the pan and cook the onion, paprika and mushrooms over medium heat until the onion has softened. Add the meat, tomato paste, stock and 1/2 cup (125 ml/4 fl oz) water. Bring to the boil, then reduce the heat and simmer for 10 minutes.
3 In a small bowl, mix the evaporated milk with the cornflour. Add to the pan and stir until the sauce boils and thickens. Sprinkle with parsley.

NUTRITION PER SERVE
Protein 35 g; Fat 4 g; Carbohydrate 8 g; Dietary Fibre 2.5 g; Cholesterol 85 mg; 900 kJ (215 cal)

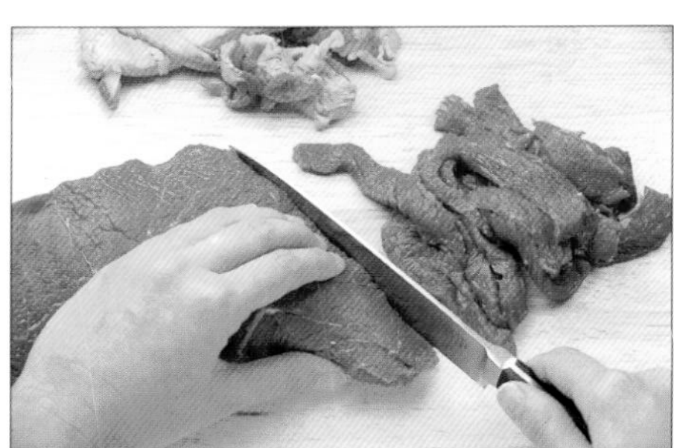
Slice the rump steak into thin strips after removing any excess fat.

Stir the onion, paprika and mushrooms until the onion has softened.

Stir the evaporated milk into the cornflour until the mixture is smooth.

DRUMSTICKS IN TOMATO AND MANGO CHUTNEY

Preparation time: 10 minutes + 2 hours marinating
Total cooking time: 20 minutes
Serves 4

8 chicken drumsticks, scored
1 tablespoon mustard powder
2 tablespoons tomato sauce
1 tablespoon sweet mango chutney
1 teaspoon Worcestershire sauce
1 tablespoon Dijon mustard
1/4 cup (30 g/1 oz) raisins
1 tablespoon oil

1 Toss the chicken in the mustard powder and season.
2 Combine the tomato sauce, chutney, Worcestershire sauce, mustard, raisins and oil. Spoon over the chicken and toss well. Marinate for at least 2 hours, turning once.
3 Cook the chicken on a hot, lightly oiled barbecue grill for about 20 minutes, or until cooked through.

NUTRITION PER SERVE
Protein 25 g; Fat 15 g; Carbohydrate 3.5 g; Dietary Fibre 0.5 g; Cholesterol 103 mg; 1005 kJ (240 cal)

HINT: Serve with toasted Turkish bread and a cool raita.

The cleanest way to toss the chicken with mustard powder is to put them in a bag.

Marinate the chicken in a shallow, non-metallic dish, turning once.

Cook the chicken on a hot flatplate until it is cooked through.

TUNA WITH LIME AND CHILLI SAUCE

Preparation time: 15 minutes
Total cooking time: 5 minutes
Serves 4

- 1/2 cup (25 g/3/4 oz) chopped and firmly packed fresh mint leaves
- 1/2 cup (25 g/3/4 oz) chopped fresh coriander leaves
- 1 teaspoon grated lime rind
- 1 tablespoon lime juice
- 1 teaspoon grated fresh ginger
- 1 jalapeño chilli, seeded and finely chopped
- 1 cup (250 g/8 oz) low-fat natural yoghurt
- 4 tuna steaks

1 Combine the mint, coriander, lime rind, lime juice, ginger and chilli in a small bowl. Fold in the yoghurt and season with salt and pepper.

2 Cook the tuna in an oiled chargrill pan or barbecue hotplate for 2 minutes each side. Serve with the sauce.

NUTRITION PER SERVE
Protein 28 g; Fat 5 g; Carbohydrate 4 g; Dietary Fibre 1 g; Cholesterol 55 mg; 800 kJ (200 Cal)

NOTE: Jalapeño chillies are smooth and thick-fleshed and are available both red and green. They are quite fiery and you can use a less powerful variety of chilli if you prefer.

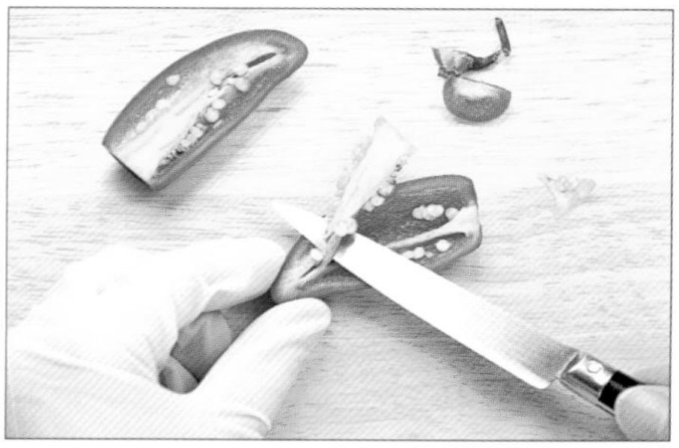

It's a good idea to wear gloves to remove the seeds from chillies, to prevent skin irritation.

Mix together the mint, coriander, lime rind, juice, ginger and chilli.

Check the taste of the sauce before seasoning with salt and black pepper.

TANDOORI CHICKEN

Preparation time: 10 minutes + 1 hour marinating
Total cooking time: 10 minutes
Serves 4

- 1/2 cup (125 g/4 oz) Greek-style plain yoghurt
- 2 tablespoons tandoori paste
- 2 cloves garlic, crushed
- 2 tablespoons lime juice
- 1 1/2 teaspoons garam masala
- 2 tablespoons finely chopped fresh coriander leaves
- 6 chicken thigh fillets

1 Combine the yoghurt, tandoori paste, garlic, lime juice, garam masala and coriander in a bowl and mix well.
2 Add the chicken, coat well, cover and refrigerate for at least 1 hour.
3 Cook the chicken on a hot, lightly oiled barbecue grill or flatplate for 5 minutes on each side, basting with the remaining marinade, until golden and cooked through. Serve with cucumber raita and naan bread.

NUTRITION PER SERVE
Protein 27 g; Fat 3.5 g; Carbohydrate 2 g; Dietary Fibre 0 g; Cholesterol 60 mg; 635 kJ (150 cal)

Mix together the yoghurt, tandoori paste, garlic, lime juice, garam masala and coriander.

Add the chicken to the marinade and leave for at least an hour.

Cook the chicken on a barbecue grill or flatplate for 5 minutes on each side.

CHARGRILLED BABY OCTOPUS

Preparation time: 15 minutes
+ overnight marinating
Total cooking time: 20 minutes
Serves 4

1 kg (2 lb) baby octopus
3/4 cup (185 ml/6 fl oz) red wine
2 tablespoons balsamic vinegar
2 tablespoons soy sauce
2 tablespoons hoisin sauce
1 clove garlic, crushed

1 Cut off the octopus heads below the eyes with a sharp knife. Discard the heads and guts. Push the beaks out with your index finger, remove and discard. Wash the octopus thoroughly under running water and drain on crumpled paper towels. If the octopus are large, cut the tentacles into quarters.

2 Put the octopus in a non-metallic bowl. Stir together the wine, vinegar, soy sauce, hoisin sauce and garlic in a jug and pour over the octopus. Toss to coat, then cover and refrigerate for several hours, or overnight.

3 Heat a chargrill pan or barbecue hotplate until very hot and then lightly oil. Drain the octopus, reserving the marinade. Cook in batches for 3–5 minutes, or until the octopus flesh turns white. Brush the marinade over the octopus during cooking. Be careful not to overcook or the octopus will be tough. Serve warm or cold. Delicious with a green salad and lime wedges.

NUTRITION PER SERVE
Protein 42.5 g; Fat 3.5 g; Carbohydrate 4 g; Dietary Fibre 1 g; Cholesterol 497.5 mg; 1060 kJ (255 Cal)

Remove and discard the head from each octopus with a sharp knife.

Push the beaks through the centre with your index finger.

Brush the octopus all over with the reserved marinade while cooking.

PORK SKEWERS ON RICE NOODLE CAKES

Preparation time: 20 minutes + 30 minutes soaking + overnight marinating
Total cooking time: 30 minutes
Serves 4

- 1 kg (2 lb) pork fillet, cut into 2 cm (3/4 inch) cubes
- 8 spring onions, cut into 3 cm (1 1/4 inch) lengths
- 2 tablespoons rice wine vinegar
- 2 teaspoons chilli bean paste
- 3 tablespoons char sui sauce
- 400 g (13 oz) fresh flat rice noodles
- 1 cup (30 g/1 oz) fresh coriander leaves, chopped
- 3 spring onions, extra, sliced
- 1 tablespoon vegetable oil
- fresh coriander sprigs, to garnish

1 Soak eight bamboo skewers in water for 30 minutes. Thread the pork and spring onion alternately on the skewers. Combine the vinegar, bean paste and char sui sauce in a shallow non-metallic dish. Add the skewers and turn to coat. Cover with plastic wrap and refrigerate overnight.
2 Drain the skewers, reserving the marinade. Heat a grill plate until very hot and cook the skewers for 1–2 minutes on each side, or until brown and cooked through. Remove and keep warm. Place the reserved marinade in a small saucepan and bring to the boil.
3 Separate the noodles with your hands, add the coriander and extra spring onion and toss together. Divide into four portions. Heat the oil in a non-stick frying pan over medium heat. Place one portion in the pan, pressing down very firmly with a spatula to form a pancake. Cook on each side for 3–4 minutes, or until golden. Remove and keep warm. Repeat with the remaining noodles.
4 To serve, place each noodle cake on a serving plate and top with two skewers. Drizzle with the marinade and garnish with the coriander sprigs.

NUTRITION PER SERVE
Protein 59.5 g; Fat 11.5 g; Carbohydrate 46.5 g; Dietary Fibre 3 g; Cholesterol 237.5 mg; 2240 kJ (535 Cal)

Thread the pork cubes and pieces of spring onion alternately onto each skewer.

Toss the coriander and spring onion through the flat rice noodles.

Press the noodles firmly with a spatula to form a pancake, then cook until golden.

CAJUN BLACKENED FISH WITH PINEAPPLE SALSA

Preparation time: 15 minutes + 20 minutes refrigeration
Total cooking time: 10 minutes
Serves 6

- 8 cm (3 inch) piece fresh pineapple, finely diced
- 6 spring onions, thinly sliced
- 2 tablespoons finely shredded fresh mint
- 1/4 cup (60 ml/ 2 fl oz) coconut vinegar
- 2 tablespoons olive oil
- 6 tablespoons ready-made Cajun spices
- 6 ling fillets
- 1/4 cup (60 g/2 oz) Greek-style plain yoghurt

1 Place the pineapple, spring onion and mint in a bowl. Season with pepper and mix together well. Just before serving, stir in the vinegar and olive oil.

2 Place the Cajun spices in a dry frying pan and dry-fry over medium heat for 1 minute, or until fragrant. Transfer the spices to a sheet of baking paper and lightly coat each side of the fish fillets, patting off any excess. Refrigerate for 20 minutes.

3 Cook the fish on a hot, lightly oiled barbecue grill or flatplate for 2–3 minutes on each side, depending on the thickness of the fish. Serve with a little yoghurt spooned over the top and the salsa on the side.

NUTRITION PER SERVE
Protein 15 g; Fat 12 g; Carbohydrate 8 g; Dietary Fibre 2 g; Cholesterol 47 mg; 883 kJ (199 cal)

Mix together the pineapple, spring onion and mint and season with pepper.

Put the spices on a sheet of baking paper and lightly coat both sides of the fish.

Cook the fish for 2–3 minutes on each side, depending on its thickness.

LAMB CHOPS WITH PINEAPPLE SALSA

Preparation time: 20 minutes
Total cooking time: 10 minutes
Serves 6

12 lamb loin chops
2 tablespoons oil
1 teaspoon cracked black pepper

PINEAPPLE SALSA
1/2 ripe pineapple (or 400 g/13 oz drained canned pineapple)
1 large red onion, finely chopped
1 fresh red chilli, seeded and diced
1 tablespoon cider or rice vinegar
1 teaspoon sugar
2 tablespoons chopped fresh mint

1 Trim the meat of excess fat and sinew. Brush the chops with oil and season with pepper.
2 To make the salsa, peel the pineapple, remove the core and eyes and dice the flesh. Toss with the onion, chilli, vinegar, sugar, salt, pepper and mint and mix well.
3 Cook the lamb chops on a hot, lightly greased barbecue flatplate or grill for 2–3 minutes each side, turning once, until just tender. Serve with the pineapple salsa.

NUTRITION PER SERVE
Protein 33 g; Fat 9 g; Carbohydrate 7 g; Dietary Fibre 2 g; Cholesterol 116 mg; 994 kJ (237 cal)

STORAGE: The salsa can be made and stored for up to a day in the fridge. Add the mint just before serving and be aware that the red onion may affect the colour of the pineapple.

Trim the lamb chops of excess fat and season, brush with oil and season with pepper.

It is a good idea to wear gloves when seeding chillies to avoid the hot juice on your fingers.

Cook the lamb chops for just 2–3 minutes on each side, turning once.

BARBECUED GARLIC CHICKEN

Preparation time: 20 minutes + marinating
Total cooking time: 10 minutes
Serves 4

6 cloves garlic, crushed
1 1/2 tablespoons cracked black peppercorns
1/2 cup (25 g/3/4 oz) chopped fresh coriander leaves and stems
4 coriander roots, chopped
1/3 cup (80 ml/2 3/4 fl oz) lime juice
1 teaspoon soft brown sugar
1 teaspoon ground turmeric
2 teaspoons light soy sauce
4 chicken breast fillets

CUCUMBER AND TOMATO SALAD
1 small green cucumber, unpeeled
1 large Roma tomato
1/4 small red onion, thinly sliced
1 small red chilli, finely chopped
2 tablespoons fresh coriander leaves
2 tablespoons lime juice
1 teaspoon soft brown sugar
1 tablespoon fish sauce

1 Blend the garlic, peppercorns, coriander, lime juice, sugar, turmeric and soy sauce in a food processor until smooth. Transfer to a bowl.
2 Remove the tenderloins from the chicken fillets. Score the top of each fillet three times. Add the fillets and tenderloins to the marinade, cover and refrigerate for 2 hours or overnight, turning the chicken occasionally.
3 To make the salad, halve the cucumber and scoop out the seeds with a teaspoon. Cut into slices. Halve the tomato lengthways and slice. Combine the cucumber, tomato, onion, chilli and coriander in a small bowl. Drizzle with the combined lime juice, sugar and fish sauce.
4 Cook the chicken on a lightly greased barbecue grill for 3 minutes on each side, or until tender. Serve the chicken immediately with the salad.

NUTRITION PER SERVE
Protein 52 g; Fat 5.5 g; Carbohydrate 6 g; Dietary Fibre 2 g; Cholesterol 110 mg; 1195 kJ (285 cal)

Add the chopped coriander roots to the other ingredients and blend until smooth.

Separate the tenderloins from the chicken fillets by pulling them away.

Use a teaspoon to scoop the seeds out of the halved cucumber.

Drizzle the combined lime juice, sugar and fish sauce over the salad ingredients.

COD WITH PAPAYA AND BLACK BEAN SALSA

Preparation time: 25 minutes
Total cooking time: 5 minutes
Serves 4

1 small red onion, finely chopped
1 papaya (about 500 g/1 lb), peeled, seeded and cubed
1 bird's-eye chilli, seeded and finely chopped
1 tablespoon salted black beans, rinsed and drained
4 blue-eye cod cutlets
2 teaspoons peanut oil
1 teaspoon sesame oil
2 teaspoons fish sauce
1 tablespoon lime juice
1 tablespoon chopped fresh coriander leaves
2 teaspoons shredded fresh mint

1 Toss together the onion, papaya, chilli and black beans.
2 Cook the cod cutlets in a lightly oiled chargrill pan or barbecue hotplate for 2 minutes each side, or until cooked to your liking.
3 Whisk together the peanut oil, sesame oil, fish sauce and lime juice. Pour over the papaya and black bean salsa and toss. Add the coriander and mint and serve immediately, at room temperature, with the fish.

NUTRITION PER SERVE
Protein 18 g; Fat 6 g; Carbohydrate 5 g; Dietary Fibre 1 g; Cholesterol 40 mg; 540 kJ (130 Cal)

NOTE: Black beans have a distinctive taste, so if you are not familiar with them, taste them before adding to the salsa. If you prefer not to add them, the salsa is equally delicious without.

VARIATION: Pawpaw can be used instead of papaya. It is a larger fruit from the same family, with yellower flesh and a less sweet flavour.

Cut the papaya in half and scoop out the seeds with a spoon.

The best way to toss the salsa, without breaking up the fruit, is with your hands.

Whisk together the oil dressing and add to the salsa just before serving.

SMOKED CHICKEN FILLETS

Preparation time: 5 minutes
Total cooking time: 25 minutes
Serves 4

4 chicken breast fillets
1 tablespoon olive oil
seasoned pepper, to taste
hickory or mesquite chips, for smoking

1 Prepare a covered barbecue grill for indirect cooking at moderate heat (normal fire). Trim the chicken of excess fat and sinew. Brush with oil and sprinkle with the seasoned pepper.
2 Spoon a pile of smoking chips (about 25) over the coals in each charcoal rail.
3 Cover the barbecue and cook the chicken for 15 minutes. Test with a sharp knife. If the juices do not run clear, cook for another 5–10 minutes until cooked through.

NUTRITION PER SERVE
Protein 56 g; Fat 10 g; Carbohydrate 0 g; Dietary Fibre 0 g; Cholesterol 125 mg; 1350 kJ (320 cal)

Brush the chicken with oil and then sprinkle with seasoned pepper.

Spoon a pile of about 25 smoking chips over the coals in each charcoal rail.

Test the chicken with a sharp knife—if it is cooked through the juices should run clear.

SCALLOPS WITH SESAME BOK CHOY

Preparation time: 10 minutes + 15 minutes marinating
Total cooking time: 10 minutes
Serves 4

24 large scallops with corals
2 tablespoons light soy sauce
1 tablespoon fish sauce
1 tablespoon honey
1 tablespoon kecap manis
grated rind and juice of 1 lime
2 teaspoons grated fresh ginger
lime wedges, to serve

SESAME BOK CHOY
1 tablespoon sesame oil
1 tablespoon sesame seeds
1 clove garlic, crushed
8 baby bok choy, halved lengthways

1 Rinse the scallops, remove the dark vein and dry with paper towels. Mix the soy and fish sauce, honey, kecap manis, lime rind and juice and ginger. Pour over the scallops, cover and refrigerate for 15 minutes. Drain, keeping the marinade.

2 To make the sesame bok choy, pour the oil onto a hot barbecue grill and add the sesame seeds and garlic. Cook, stirring, for 1 minute, or until the seeds are golden. Arrange the bok choy in a single layer on the hot plate and pour over the reserved marinade. Cook for 3–4 minutes, turning once, until tender. Remove and keep warm.

3 Wipe clean the grill, brush with oil and reheat. Add the scallops and cook, turning, for about 2 minutes, or until they become opaque. Serve on top of the bok choy, with the lime wedges.

NUTRITION PER SERVE
Protein 15 g; Fat 5 g; Carbohydrate 10 g; Dietary Fibre 1 g; Cholesterol 25 mg; 670 kJ (160 cal)

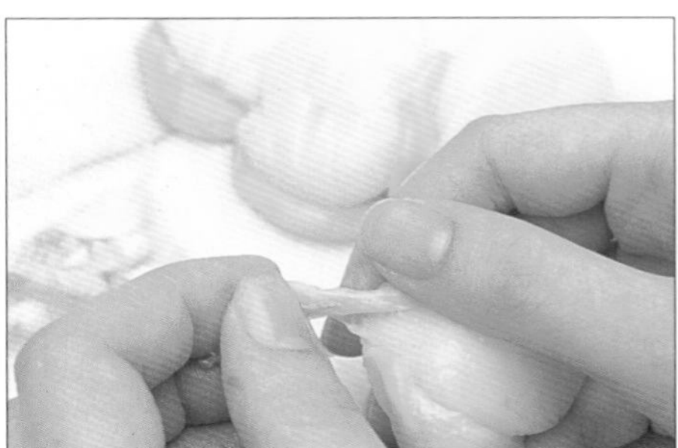
Rinse the scallops and then remove their dark veins and dry with paper towels.

Arrange the halved bok choy in a single layer on the flatplate.

Cook the scallops for about 2 minutes, turning often, until they are opaque.

PORK ROLLS WITH ROASTED CAPSICUM

Preparation time: 40 minutes
Total cooking time: 30 minutes
Serves 4

SAUCE
3/4 cup (185 ml/6 fl oz) beef stock
2 teaspoons soy sauce
2 tablespoons red wine
2 teaspoons wholegrain mustard
2 teaspoons cornflour

1 red capsicum
4 x 150 g (5 oz) lean pork leg steaks
1/3 cup (90 g/3 oz) ricotta
2 spring onions, finely chopped
1 clove garlic, crushed
75 g (2 1/2 oz) rocket
4 small lean slices prosciutto (about 35 g/1 1/4 oz)
cooking oil spray

1 To make the sauce, put the beef stock, soy sauce, red wine and mustard in a pan. Blend the cornflour with 1 tablespoon water and add to the pan. Stir until the mixture boils.
2 Cut the capsicum into quarters and remove the seeds and membrane. Grill until the skin blisters and blackens. Cool under a damp tea towel, peel and cut the flesh into thin strips.
3 Flatten each steak into a thin square between 2 sheets of plastic, using a rolling pin or mallet. Combine the ricotta, onion and garlic in a bowl, then spread evenly over the pork. Top with a layer of rocket and prosciutto. Place a quarter of the capsicum at one end and roll up to enclose the capsicum. Tie with string or secure with toothpicks at even intervals.
4 Spray a non-stick pan with oil and fry the pork rolls over medium heat for 5 minutes, or until well browned. Add the sauce to the pan and simmer over low heat for 10–15 minutes, or until the rolls are cooked. Remove the string or toothpicks. Slice and serve with the sauce.

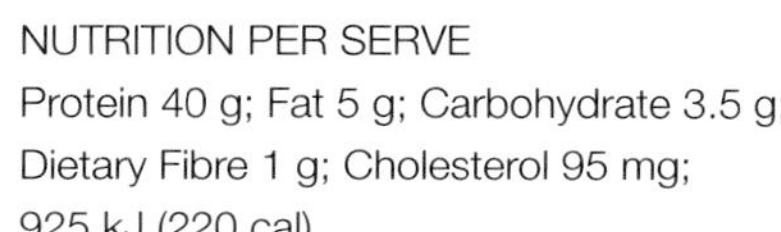

NUTRITION PER SERVE
Protein 40 g; Fat 5 g; Carbohydrate 3.5 g; Dietary Fibre 1 g; Cholesterol 95 mg; 925 kJ (220 cal)

Flatten the pork between two pieces of plastic wrap, using a rolling pin or mallet.

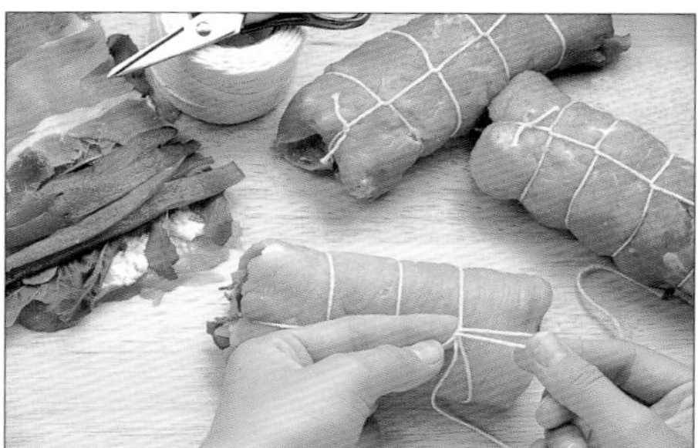

Secure the pork rolls with string or toothpicks at even intervals.

Add the sauce to the pan and simmer over low heat until cooked through.

LAMB BURGER WITH WEDGES

Preparation time: 30 minutes
Total cooking time: 1 hour
Serves 4

1 red capsicum
1 yellow capsicum
1 green capsicum
400 g (13 oz) baking potatoes (pontiac or desiree)
garlic oil spray
300 g (10 oz) lean lamb mince
2 teaspoons chopped fresh thyme
2 tablespoons chopped fresh parsley
2 tomatoes (140 g/4$\frac{1}{2}$ oz), seeded and finely chopped
1 large onion, finely chopped
$\frac{1}{3}$ cup (25 g/$\frac{3}{4}$ oz) fresh breadcrumbs
1 egg white, lightly beaten
4 slices low-fat cheese
1 large red onion, thinly sliced
2 teaspoons olive oil
4 hamburger buns
40 g (1$\frac{1}{4}$ oz) rocket

1 Cut the capsicums into quarters and remove the membranes and seeds. Grill, skin-side up, until the skin blackens and blisters. Place in a bowl and cover with plastic wrap. When cool enough to handle, peel off the skin and cut the capsicums into strips.
2 Preheat the oven to moderately hot 200°C (400°F/Gas 6). Line a baking tray with foil. Cut the potatoes into medium wedges. Spray well with the oil spray, then season and toss. Lay out evenly on the baking tray. Bake for 40 minutes, or until crisp and golden, turning once.
3 Meanwhile, combine the mince, thyme, parsley, tomato, onion, breadcrumbs, egg white and 1 teaspoon ground black pepper. Form into four even-sized patties. Heat a non-stick frying pan over medium heat and cook the patties on each side for 5 minutes, or until cooked. Put a slice of cheese on top to melt slightly. Remove from the pan. Cook the onion in the olive oil for 4–5 minutes over medium heat until softened a little. Cut the buns in half and toast each side until crisp.

4 To assemble, layer the bun with a little rocket, the patty with cheese, onion, one strip each of red, yellow and green capsicum, and top with more rocket and the top of the bun. Cut in half and serve with wedges.

NUTRITION PER SERVE
Protein 34.5 g; Fat 14 g; Carbohydrate 52 g; Dietary Fibre 5.5 g; Cholesterol 65.5 mg; 1995 kJ (475 Cal)

Peel the blackened and blistered skin from the capsicum.

Using your hands, form the mince mixture into even-sized patties.

SWEET CHILLI OCTOPUS

Preparation time: 15 minutes
Total cooking time: 5 minutes
Serves 4

1.5 kg (3 lb) baby octopus
1 cup (250 ml/8 fl oz) sweet chilli sauce
1/3 cup (80 ml/2 3/4 fl oz) lime juice
1/3 cup (80 ml/2 3/4 fl oz) fish sauce
1/3 cup (60 g/2 oz) soft brown sugar
lime wedges, to serve

1 Cut off the octopus heads, below the eyes, with a sharp knife. Discard the heads and guts. Push the beaks out with your index finger, remove and discard. Wash the octopus thoroughly under running water and drain on crumpled paper towels. If the octopus tentacles are large, cut into quarters.
2 Mix together the sweet chilli sauce, lime juice, fish sauce and sugar.
3 Cook the octopus on a very hot, lightly oiled barbecue grill or flatplate, turning often, for 3–4 minutes, or until it just changes colour. Brush with a quarter of the sauce during cooking. Do not overcook the octopus or it will toughen. Serve immediately with the remaining sauce and lime wedges.

NUTRITION PER SERVE
Protein 43 g; Fat 11 g; Carbohydrate 25 g; Dietary Fibre 2.5 g; Cholesterol 500 mg; 1543 kJ (370 cal)

Push the beak upwards with your index finger to remove it.

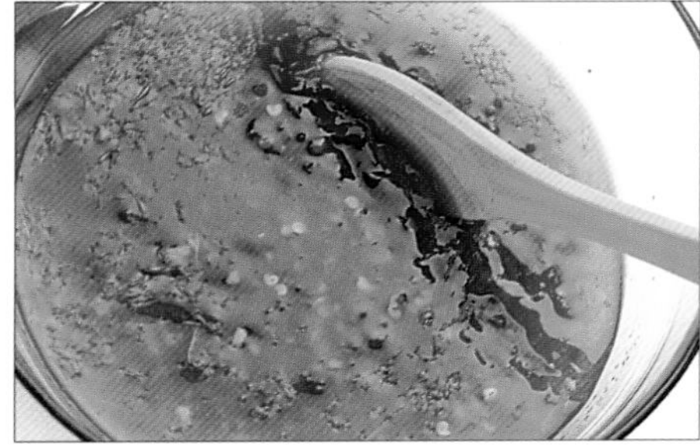

Mix together the sweet chilli sauce, lime juice, fish sauce and sugar.

Cook the octopus just until it changes colour, otherwise it will be tough.

YAKITORI

Preparation time: 20 minutes
+ soaking
Total cooking time: 10 minutes
Makes 25 skewers

- 1 kg (2 lb) chicken thigh fillets
- 1/2 cup (125 ml/4 fl oz) sake
- 3/4 cup (185 ml/6 fl oz) shoyu (Japanese soy sauce)
- 1/2 cup (125 ml/4 fl oz) mirin
- 2 tablespoons sugar
- 10 spring onions, diagonally cut into 2 cm (3/4 inch) pieces

1 Soak 25 wooden skewers in water for about 20 minutes to prevent burning. Drain and set aside.
2 Cut the chicken thigh fillets into bite-sized pieces. Combine the sake, shoyu, mirin and sugar in a small pan. Bring the mixture to the boil and then set aside.
3 Thread the chicken pieces onto the wooden skewers alternately with the spring onion pieces. Place the chicken skewers on a foil-lined tray and cook them under a preheated grill or on a barbecue hotplate, turning and brushing frequently with the sauce, for 7–8 minutes, or until the chicken is cooked through. Serve immediately, garnished with a few spring onion pieces.

NUTRITION PER SKEWER
Protein 9.5 g; Fat 1 g; Carbohydrate 3 g; Dietary Fibre 0 g; Cholesterol 20 mg; 270 kJ (64 cal)

NOTE: In Japan, Yakitori is usually served as a snack with beer. The addition of steamed rice and your favourite vegetables turns these delicious kebabs into a satisfying meal.

Use a sharp knife to cut the chicken thigh fillets into bite-sized pieces.

Thread the chicken pieces and spring onion alternately onto the skewers.

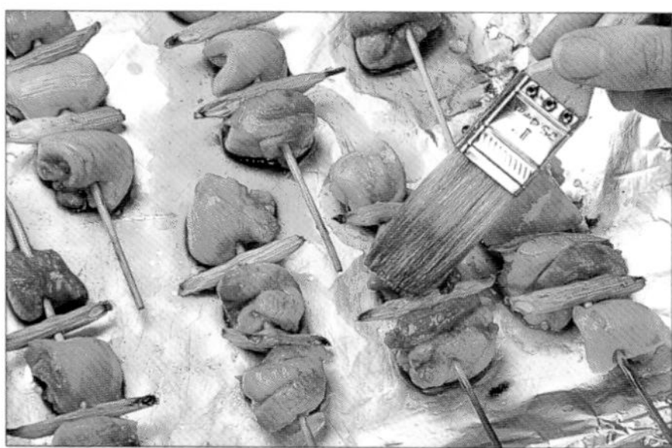

Frequently brush the chicken with the sauce as it cooks.

LAMB CUTLETS WITH CANNELLINI BEAN PUREE

Preparation time: 30 minutes + 1 hour refrigeration
Total cooking time: 20 minutes
Serves 4

8 lamb cutlets
4 cloves garlic
1 tablespoon chopped fresh rosemary
2 teaspoons olive oil
2 x 400 g (13 oz) cans cannellini beans, drained
1 teaspoon ground cumin
1/2 cup (125 ml/4 fl oz) lemon juice
cooking oil spray
2 tablespoons balsamic vinegar

1 Trim the cutlets of excess fat from the outside edge and scrape the fat away from the bones. Place in a single layer in a shallow dish. Thinly slice 2 garlic cloves and mix with the rosemary, oil and 1/2 teaspoon salt and cracked black pepper. Pour over the meat, cover and refrigerate for 1 hour.
2 Rinse the beans and purée with the remaining garlic, the cumin and half the lemon juice in a food processor. Transfer to a pan, then set aside.
3 Lightly spray a non-stick frying pan with oil and cook the cutlets over medium heat for 1–2 minutes on each side. Add the vinegar and cook for 1 minute, turning to coat. Remove the cutlets and cover to keep warm. Add the remaining lemon juice to the pan and simmer for 2–3 minutes, or until the sauce thickens slightly. Warm the purée over medium heat and serve with the cutlets.

NUTRITION PER SERVE
Protein 30 g; Fat 8 g; Carbohydrate 45 g; Dietary Fibre 3.5 g; Cholesterol 50 mg; 1560 kJ (375 Cal)

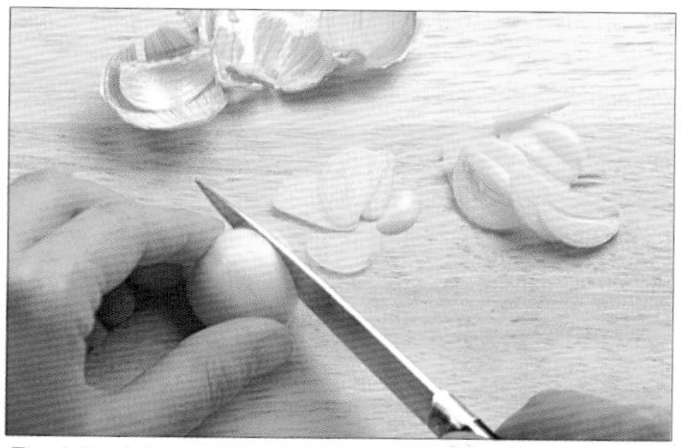

Peel 2 of the garlic cloves and thinly slice with a sharp knife.

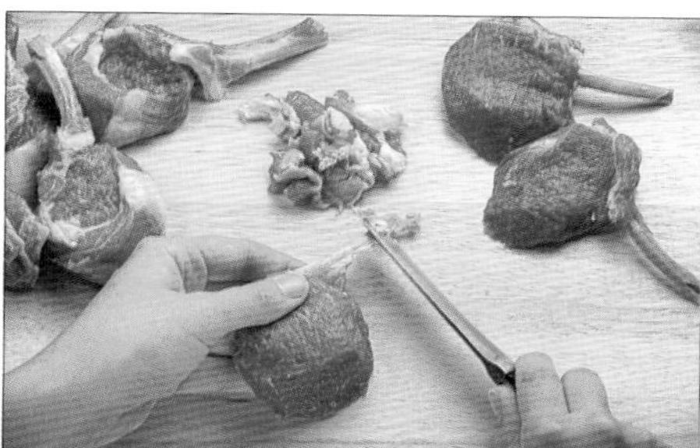

Trim all the excess fat from the cutlets, scraping any away from the bones.

After cooking the cutlets lightly on each side, add the vinegar to the pan.

pasta, gnocchi, rice & noodles

PASTA PUTTANESCA

Preparation time: 15 minutes
Total cooking time: 20 minutes
Serves 4–6

- 500 g (1 lb) spaghetti or fettucine
- 2 tablespoons olive oil
- 3 cloves garlic, crushed
- 2 tablespoons chopped fresh parsley
- 1/4–1/2 teaspoon chilli flakes or chilli powder
- 2 x 425 g (14 oz) cans crushed tomatoes
- 1 tablespoon capers
- 3 anchovy fillets, chopped
- 3 tablespoons black olives

1 Cook the spaghetti or fettuccine in a large pan of rapidly boiling salted water until *al dente*. Drain and return to the pan to keep warm.

2 Meanwhile, heat the oil in a heavy-based frying pan. Add the garlic, parsley and chilli flakes and cook, stirring, for 1 minute over medium heat.

3 Add the crushed tomatoes and stir to combine. Reduce the heat and simmer, covered, for 5 minutes.

4 Add the capers, anchovies and olives and cook, stirring, for 5 minutes. Season with black pepper. Add the sauce to the pasta and toss together gently. Serve immediately.

NUTRITION PER SERVE (6)
Protein 11 g; Fat 7 g; Carbohydrate 63 g; Dietary Fibre 6 g; Cholesterol 0 mg; 1549 kJ (370 Cal)

HINT: If you can't find cans of crushed tomatoes, used canned whole tomatoes—simply chop in the can with a pair of kitchen scissors.

Cook the pasta in boiling water, then drain and return to the pan to keep warm.

Cook the garlic, parsley and chilli flakes over medium heat for 1 minute.

Add the crushed tomatoes to the garlic, parsley and chilli flakes.

Add the capers, anchovies and olives and stir for 5 minutes.

TUNA WITH CORIANDER NOODLES

Preparation time: 15 minutes
Total cooking time: 10 minutes
Serves 4

1/4 cup (60 ml/2 fl oz) lime juice
2 tablespoons fish sauce
2 tablespoons sweet chilli sauce
2 teaspoons grated palm sugar
1 teaspoon sesame oil
1 clove garlic, finely chopped
1 tablespoon virgin olive oil
4 tuna steaks
200 g (6 1/2 oz) dried thin wheat noodles
6 spring onions, thinly sliced
3/4 cup (25 g/3/4 oz) chopped fresh coriander leaves
lime wedges, to garnish

1 To make the dressing, place the lime juice, fish sauce, chilli sauce, sugar, sesame oil and garlic in a small bowl and mix together.
2 Heat the olive oil in a chargrill pan or on a barbecue hotplate. Add the tuna steaks and cook over high heat for 2 minutes each side, or until cooked to your liking. Transfer the steaks to a warm plate, cover and keep warm.
3 Place the noodles in a large saucepan of lightly salted, rapidly boiling water and return to the boil. Cook for 4 minutes, or until the noodles are tender. Drain well. Add half the dressing and half the spring onion and coriander to the noodles and gently toss together.
4 Either cut the tuna into even cubes or slice it into even pieces.
5 Place the noodles on serving plates and top with the tuna. Mix the remaining dressing with the spring onion and coriander and drizzle over the tuna. Garnish with lime wedges.

NUTRITION PER SERVE
Protein 32 g; Fat 10 g; Carbohydrate 5 g; Dietary Fibre 1 g; Cholesterol 105 mg; 1030 kJ (245 Cal)

Cook the tuna steaks in a chargrill pan until cooked to your liking.

Cook the noodles in lightly salted water until they are tender.

Combine the remaining dressing with the spring onion and coriander.

PRAWN FRIED RICE

Preparation time: 20 minutes
Total cooking time: 15 minutes
Serves 6

- oil, for cooking
- 4 egg whites, lightly beaten
- 2 cloves garlic, crushed
- 350 g (12 oz) raw prawns, peeled, deveined and halved lengthways
- 100 g ($3\frac{1}{2}$ oz) cooked chicken, shredded
- $\frac{1}{2}$ cup (80 g/$2\frac{3}{4}$ oz) frozen peas
- 180 g (6 oz) sliced ham, cut into small strips
- 1 red capsicum, diced
- 4 spring onions, sliced
- 4 cups (750 g/$1\frac{1}{2}$ lb) cooked white and wild rice blend (see HINT)
- $1\frac{1}{2}$ tablespoons soy sauce
- 3 teaspoons fish sauce
- $1\frac{1}{2}$ teaspoons soft brown sugar

1 Heat 2 teaspoons of the oil in a wok and pour in the egg white. Cook over low heat, stirring until the egg is just cooked and slightly scrambled, then remove and set aside.

2 Reheat the wok, add a little more oil and stir-fry the garlic, prawns, chicken, peas, ham and capsicum for 3–4 minutes, or until the prawns are cooked through.

3 Add the spring onion, rice, soy and fish sauces and sugar and toss for 30 seconds, or until heated through. Add the egg, toss lightly and serve.

NUTRITION PER SERVE
Protein 35 g; Fat 3 g; Carbohydrate 105 g; Dietary Fibre 4 g; Cholesterol 120 mg; 2500 kJ (600 cal)

HINT: You will need to cook $1\frac{1}{3}$ cups (260 g/8 oz) rice to get 4 cupfuls. For fried rice it is best to steam or boil your rice a day in advance and leave it in the fridge overnight. This allows the grains to separate.

Stir the egg white over low heat until just cooked and slightly scrambled.

Stir-fry the garlic, prawns, chicken, peas, ham and capsicum.

When the prawns are cooked through, add the spring onion, rice, sauces and sugar.

PASTA WITH ARTICHOKES AND CHARGRILLED CHICKEN

Preparation time: 10 minutes
Total cooking time: 30 minutes
Serves 6

1 tablespoon olive oil
3 chicken breast fillets
500 g (1 lb) pasta
8 slices prosciutto
280 g (9 oz) jar artichokes in oil, drained and quartered, oil reserved
150 g (5 oz) semi-dried tomatoes, thinly sliced
90 g (3 oz) baby rocket leaves
2–3 tablespoons balsamic vinegar

1 Lightly brush a chargrill or frying pan with the oil and heat over high heat. Cook the chicken for 6–8 minutes each side, or until cooked through. Thinly slice and set aside.

2 Cook the pasta in a large pan of rapidly boiling salted water until *al dente*. Drain and return to the pan to keep warm. Meanwhile, place the prosciutto on a grill tray and cook under a hot grill for 2 minutes each side, or until crisp. Cool slightly and break into pieces. Combine the pasta with the chicken, prosciutto, artichokes, tomato and rocket in a bowl and toss. Whisk together 1/4 cup (60 ml/2 fl oz) of the reserved artichoke oil and the balsamic vinegar and toss through the pasta mixture. Season and serve.

NUTRITION PER SERVE
Protein 30 g; Fat 9 g; Carbohydrate 51 g; Dietary Fibre 4 g; Cholesterol 103 mg; 1705 kJ (410 cal)

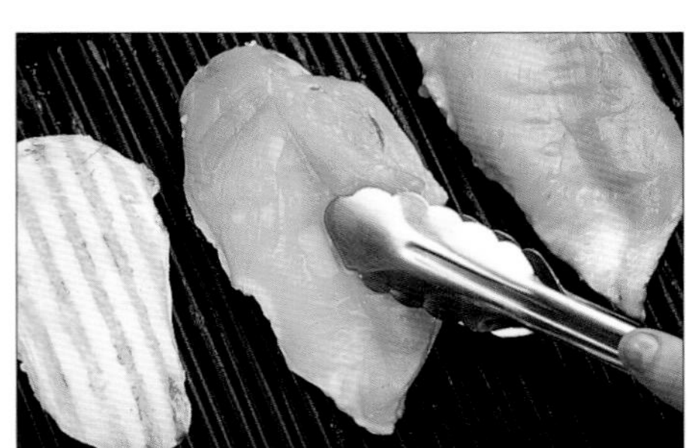

You can either fry or chargrill the chicken breast fillets, then thinly slice.

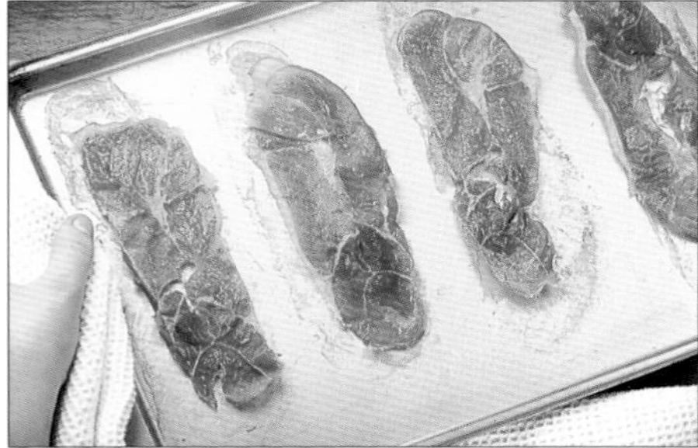

Cook the prosciutto under a hot grill until crisp. Allow to cool, then break into pieces.

PENNE WITH RICOTTA AND BASIL SAUCE

Preparation time: 20 minutes
Total cooking time: 15 minutes
Serves 4

2 bacon rashers
2 teaspoons olive oil
2–3 cloves garlic, crushed
1 onion, finely chopped
2 spring onions, finely chopped
1/2 cup (30 g/1 oz) finely chopped fresh basil
250 g (8 oz) ricotta
325 g (11 oz) penne
8 cherry tomatoes, halved

1 Remove the fat and rind from the bacon and chop roughly. Heat the oil in a pan, add the bacon, garlic, onion and spring onion and stir over medium heat for 5 minutes, or until cooked. Remove from the heat, stir in the chopped basil and ricotta, and beat until smooth.

2 Meanwhile, cook the pasta in a large pan of rapidly boiling salted water for 10 minutes, or until *al dente*. Just prior to draining the pasta, add about a cup of the pasta water to the ricotta mixture to thin the sauce. Add more water if you prefer an even thinner sauce. Season well.

3 Drain the pasta and stir the sauce and tomato halves into the pasta.

NUTRITION PER SERVE
Protein 20 g; Fat 10 g; Carbohydrate 65 g; Dietary Fibre 5 g; Cholesterol 40 mg; 1885 kJ (450 Cal)

Remove from the heat and stir in the ricotta and chopped basil.

Bring a large pan of salted water to a rapid boil before adding the pasta.

Thin the ricotta mixture with about a cup of the water from the cooked pasta.

UDON NOODLE STIR-FRY

Preparation time: 15 minutes
Total cooking time: 10 minutes
Serves 4

500 g (1 lb) fresh udon noodles
1 tablespoon oil
6 spring onions, cut into short lengths
3 cloves garlic, crushed
1 tablespoon grated fresh ginger
2 carrots, cut into short lengths
150 g (5 oz) snow peas, cut in half on the diagonal
100 g (3 1/2 oz) bean sprouts
500 g (1 lb) choy sum, cut into short lengths
2 tablespoons Japanese soy sauce
2 tablespoons mirin
2 tablespoons kecap manis
2 sheets roasted nori, cut into thin strips

1 Bring a saucepan of water to the boil, add the noodles and cook for 5 minutes, or until tender and not clumped together. Drain and rinse under hot water.

2 Heat the oil in a wok until hot, then add the spring onion, garlic and ginger. Stir-fry over high heat for 1–2 minutes, or until soft. Add the carrot, snow peas and 1 tablespoon water, toss well, cover and cook for 1–2 minutes, or until the vegetables are just tender.

3 Add the noodles, bean sprouts, choy sum, soy sauce, mirin and kecap manis, then toss until the choy sum is wilted and coated with the sauce. Stir in the nori just before serving.

NUTRITION PER SERVE
Protein 25 g; Fat 7.5 g; Carbohydrate 95 g; Dietary Fibre 13 g; Cholesterol 0 mg; 2330 kJ (557 cal)

Cut the roasted nori sheets into very thin strips. It is available from Asian speciality shops.

Cook the udon noodles until they are tender and not clumped together.

Stir-fry the greens, noodles and sauces until the choy sum is wilted and coated with sauce.

SWEET AND SOUR FISH WITH HOKKIEN NOODLES

Preparation time: 20 minutes
Total cooking time: 20 minutes
Serves 4

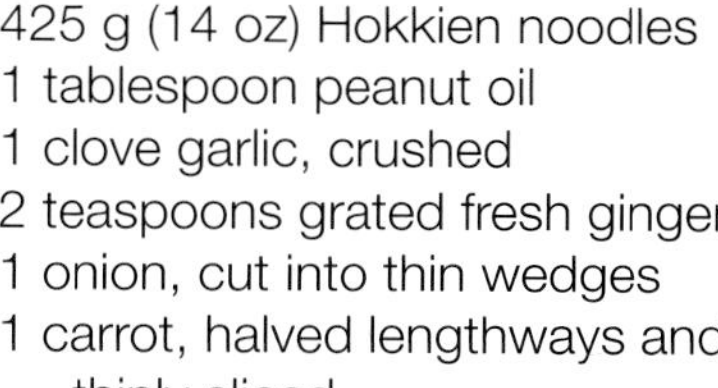

425 g (14 oz) Hokkien noodles
1 tablespoon peanut oil
1 clove garlic, crushed
2 teaspoons grated fresh ginger
1 onion, cut into thin wedges
1 carrot, halved lengthways and thinly sliced
1/2 red capsicum, cut into thin strips
1/2 green capsicum, cut into thin strips
1 celery stick, thinly sliced
1/2 cup (60 g/2 oz) plain flour
1/4 cup (45 g/1 1/2 oz) rice flour
1 teaspoon caster sugar
1/2 teaspoon ground white pepper
500 g (1 lb) firm white fish fillets (ling, flake, snapper), cut into 3–4 cm (1 1/4–1 1/2 inch) cubes
1 egg, beaten with 1 tablespoon water
oil, to deep-fry
2 spring onions, sliced diagonally

SAUCE
1/4 cup (60 ml/2 fl oz) rice vinegar
1 tablespoon cornflour
3 tablespoons tomato sauce
2 tablespoons sugar
2 teaspoons light soy sauce
1/4 cup (60 ml/2 fl oz) pineapple juice
1 tablespoon dry sherry
2 tablespoons vegetable stock

1 Place the noodles in a heatproof bowl, cover with boiling water and soak for 1 minute. Drain.
2 To make the sauce, combine the vinegar and cornflour, then stir in the tomato sauce, sugar, soy sauce, pineapple juice, sherry, stock and 3/4 cup (185 ml/6 fl oz) water.
3 Heat a wok over medium heat, add the oil and swirl to coat the side. Cook the garlic and ginger for 30 seconds. Add the onion, carrot, red and green capsicum and celery and stir-fry for 3–4 minutes. Add the sauce to the wok, increase the heat to high and stir-fry for 1–2 minutes, or until thickened. Remove from the heat and keep warm.
4 Combine the flours, sugar and white pepper in a medium bowl. Dip each piece of fish in the egg, then coat in the flour mix, shaking off any excess. Fill a deep heavy-based saucepan one-third full of oil and heat to 180°C (350°F), or until a cube of bread browns in 15 seconds. Deep-fry the fish in batches for 3 minutes, or until cooked and golden. Drain on paper towels and keep warm.
5 Return the wok with the sauce to medium heat, add the noodles and toss together for 3–4 minutes, or until heated through. Gently toss the fish through, top with the spring onion and serve immediately.

NUTRITION PER SERVE
Protein 41.5 g; Fat 10 g; Carbohydrate 98.5 g; Dietary Fibre 4.5 g; Cholesterol 138 mg; 2760 kJ (660 Cal)

Add the sauce to the wok and stir-fry until the sauce thickens.

LASAGNE

Preparation time: 40 minutes
Total cooking time: 1 hour 35 minutes
Serves 8

2 teaspoons olive oil
1 large onion, chopped
2 carrots, finely chopped
2 celery stalks, finely chopped
2 zucchini, finely chopped
2 cloves garlic, crushed
500 g (1 lb) lean beef mince
2 x 400 g (13 oz) cans crushed tomatoes
1/2 cup (125 ml/4 fl oz) beef stock
2 tablespoons tomato paste
2 teaspoons dried oregano
375 g (12 oz) lasagne sheets

CHEESE SAUCE
3 cups (750 ml/24 fl oz) skim milk
1/3 cup (40 g/1 1/4 oz) cornflour
100 g (3 1/2 oz) reduced-fat cheese, grated

1 Heat the olive oil in a large non-stick frying pan. Add the onion and cook for 5 minutes, until soft. Add the carrot, celery and zucchini and cook, stirring constantly, for 5 minutes, or until the vegetables are soft. Add the crushed garlic and cook for another minute. Add the beef mince and cook over high heat, stirring, until well browned. Break up any lumps of meat with a wooden spoon.
2 Add the crushed tomato, beef stock, tomato paste and dried oregano to the pan and stir to thoroughly combine. Bring the mixture to the boil, then reduce the heat and simmer gently, partially covered, for 20 minutes, stirring occasionally to prevent the mixture sticking to the pan.
3 Preheat the oven to moderate 180°C (350°F/Gas 4). Spread a little of the meat sauce into the base of a 23 x 30 cm (9 x 12 inch) ovenproof dish. Arrange a layer of lasagne sheets in the dish, breaking some of the sheets, if necessary, to fit in neatly.
4 Spread half the meat sauce over the top to cover evenly. Cover with another layer of lasagne sheets, a layer of meat sauce, then a final layer of lasagne sheets.
5 To make the cheese sauce, blend a little of the milk with the cornflour, to form a smooth paste, in a small pan. Gradually blend in the remaining milk and stir constantly over low heat until the mixture boils and thickens. Remove from the heat and stir in the grated cheese until melted. Spread evenly over the top of the lasagne and bake for 1 hour.
6 Check the lasagne after 25 minutes. If the top is browning too quickly, cover loosely with non-stick baking paper or foil. Take care when removing the baking paper or foil that the topping does not come away with the paper. For serving, cut the lasagne into eight portions and garnish with fresh herbs.

NUTRITION PER SERVE
Protein 15 g; Fat 12 g; Carbohydrate 50 g; Dietary Fibre 5 g; Cholesterol 10 mg; 1885 kJ (450 cal)

STORAGE: Can be frozen for up to 2–3 months. When required, thaw overnight in the refrigerator, then reheat, covered with foil, for about 30 minutes in a moderate oven.

Chop the garlic and crush using the flat side of a large knife.

Add the vegetables to the pan and stir constantly until soft.

When you add the meat, break up any lumps with a wooden spoon.

Spread a little of the meat sauce over the base and cover evenly with lasagne sheets.

Remove the pan from the heat and stir in the cheese until melted.

Spread the cheese sauce evenly over the top of the lasagne.

DEEP-FRIED TOFU WITH HOKKIEN NOODLES

Preparation time: 10 minutes
Total cooking time: 5 minutes
Serves 4

- 100 g (3½ oz) deep-fried tofu puffs (see HINT)
- 2 tablespoons oil
- 1 onion, sliced
- 1 red capsicum, cut into squares
- 3 cloves garlic, crushed
- 2 teaspoons grated fresh ginger
- ¾ cup (120 g/4 oz) small chunks fresh pineapple
- 500 g (1 lb) thin Hokkien noodles, gently pulled apart
- ¼ cup (60 ml/2 fl oz) pineapple juice
- ¼ cup (60 ml/2 fl oz) hoisin sauce
- ¼ cup (15 g/½ oz) roughly chopped fresh coriander

1 Slice the tofu puffs into three, then cut each slice into two or three pieces.
2 Heat the wok until very hot, add the oil and stir-fry the onion and capsicum for 1–2 minutes, or until beginning to soften. Add the garlic and ginger, stir-fry for 1 minute, then add the tofu and stir-fry for 2 minutes.
3 Add the pineapple chunks and noodles and toss until the mixture is combined and heated through. Add the pineapple juice, hoisin sauce and chopped coriander and toss to combine. Serve immediately.

NUTRITION PER SERVE
Protein 10 g; Fat 15 g; Carbohydrate 65 g; Dietary Fibre 3.5 g; Cholesterol 0 mg; 1830 kJ (435 cal)

HINT: Deep-fried tofu puffs are available from the refrigerated section in Asian grocery stores and some supermarkets. They have a very different texture to ordinary tofu.

Use your fingers to gently separate the Hokkien noodles before cooking.

Slice the tofu puffs into three, then cut into smaller pieces.

Stir-fry the onion and capsicum until they are beginning to soften.

CHIANG MAI NOODLES

Preparation time: 20 minutes
Total cooking time: 15 minutes
Serves 4

500 g (1 lb) fresh egg noodles
1 tablespoon oil
3 French or Asian shallots, peeled and chopped
6 cloves garlic, chopped
2 teaspoons finely chopped red chilli, optional
1–2 tablespoons red curry paste
350 g (11 oz) lean chicken, thinly sliced
1 carrot, cut into fine, thin strips
2 tablespoons fish sauce
2 teaspoons soft brown sugar
3 spring onions, thinly sliced
1/4 cup (7 g/1/4 oz) fresh coriander leaves

1 Cook the noodles in a wok or pan of rapidly boiling water for 2–3 minutes, or until they are just tender. Drain and keep warm.
2 Heat the oil in a wok or large frying pan until it is very hot. Add the shallots, garlic, chilli and curry paste, and stir-fry for 2 minutes, or until the mixture is fragrant. Add the chicken in two batches and cook for 3 minutes, or until the chicken changes colour.
3 Return all of the chicken to the wok. Add the carrot, fish sauce and brown sugar, and bring to the boil. Divide the noodles between serving bowls and mix in portions of the chicken mixture and spring onion. Top with the coriander leaves. Serve immediately.

NUTRITION PER SERVE
Protein 37 g; Fat 10 g; Carbohydrate 92 g; Dietary Fibre 4.5 g; Cholesterol 67 mg; 2565 kJ (612 cal)

HINT: This dish must be served as soon as it is cooked or the noodles and vegetables will go soggy.

Use a sharp knife to peel and finely chop the French shallots.

Cook the noodles in a wok or pan of rapidly boiling water until just tender.

Place all the chicken back into the wok. Add carrot, fish sauce and brown sugar.

LINGUINE WITH BACON, MUSHROOMS AND PEAS

Preparation time: 20 minutes
Total cooking time: 25 minutes
Serves 4

3 bacon rashers
2 teaspoons olive oil
2–3 cloves garlic, crushed
1 red onion, chopped
185 g (6 oz) field mushrooms, sliced
1/3 cup (20 g/3/4 oz) chopped fresh parsley
1 cup (150 g/5 oz) peas
1 1/2 cups (375 ml/12 fl oz) low-fat light evaporated milk
2 teaspoons cornflour
325 g (11 oz) linguine
25 g (3/4 oz) Parmesan shavings

1 Remove the fat and rind from the bacon and chop roughly. Heat the oil in a medium pan, add the garlic, onion and bacon and cook over low heat for 5 minutes, stirring frequently, until the onion and bacon are soft. Add the sliced mushrooms and cook, stirring, for another 5 minutes, or until soft.

2 Add the parsley, peas and milk to the pan. Mix the cornflour with 1 tablespoon of water until smooth, add to the mixture and stir over medium heat until slightly thickened.

3 Cook the pasta in a large pan of rapidly boiling salted water until *al dente*. Drain well and serve with the hot sauce and Parmesan shavings.

NUTRITION PER SERVE
Protein 30 g; Fat 7 g; Carbohydrate 80 g; Dietary Fibre 9 g; Cholesterol 25 mg; 2085 kJ (500 cal)

NOTE: Parmesan adds a nice flavour to this dish, but leave it out if you are wanting a meal with a very low fat content.

Discard the fat and rind from the bacon and chop the meat roughly into strips.

When the onion is softened, add the sliced mushrooms and stir while cooking.

Stir the vegetable mixture until the liquid has slightly thickened.

SILVERBEET PARCELS

Preparation time: 40 minutes
Total cooking time: 1 hour
Serves 6

2 cups (500 ml/16 fl oz) vegetable stock
1 tablespoon olive oil
1 onion, chopped
2 cloves garlic, crushed
1 red capsicum, chopped
250 g (8 oz) mushrooms, chopped
1/2 cup (110 g/3 1/2 oz) arborio rice
60 g (2 oz) Cheddar, grated
1/4 cup (15 g/1/2 oz) shredded fresh basil
6 large silverbeet leaves
2 x 400 g (13 oz) cans chopped tomatoes
1 tablespoon balsamic vinegar
1 teaspoon soft brown sugar

1 Heat the vegetable stock in a pan and maintain at simmering point. Heat the oil in a large pan, add the onion and garlic and cook until the onion has softened. Add the capsicum, mushrooms and rice and stir until well combined. Gradually add 1/2 cup (125 ml/4 fl oz) hot stock, stirring until the liquid has been absorbed. Continue to add the stock, a little at a time, stirring constantly for 20–25 minutes, or until the rice is creamy and tender (you may not need all the stock, or you may need to add a little water if you run out). Remove from the heat, add the cheese and basil and season well.
2 Trim the stalks from the silverbeet and cook the leaves, a few at a time, in a large pan of boiling water for 30 seconds, or until wilted. Drain on a tea towel. Using a sharp knife, cut away any tough white veins from the centre of the leaves without cutting them in half. If necessary, overlap the two sides to make a flat surface. Place a portion of mushroom filling in the centre of each leaf, fold in the sides and roll up carefully. Tie with string.
3 Put the tomato, balsamic vinegar and sugar in a large, deep non-stick frying pan and stir to combine. Add the silverbeet parcels, cover and simmer for 10 minutes. Remove the string and serve with tomato sauce.

NUTRITION PER SERVE
Protein 7.5 g; Fat 6 g; Carbohydrate 20 g; Dietary Fibre 4 g; Cholesterol 7 mg; 725 kJ (175 cal)

Add the stock, a little at a time, until the rice is tender and has absorbed the stock.

Using a sharp knife, cut away the white veins from the centre of the leaves.

Place the filling in the centre of each leaf, fold in the sides and roll up into parcels.

SWEET CHILLI CHICKEN

Preparation time: 10 minutes
Total cooking time: 10 minutes
Serves 4–6

375 g (12 oz) Hokkien noodles
4 chicken thigh fillets, cut into small pieces (see NOTE)
1–2 tablespoons sweet chilli sauce
2 teaspoons fish sauce
1 tablespoon oil
100 g ($3\frac{1}{2}$ oz) baby sweet corn, halved lengthways
150 g (5 oz) sugar snap peas
1 tablespoon lime juice

1 Place the noodles in a large bowl, cover with boiling water and gently pull apart with a fork. Leave for 5 minutes, then drain.
2 Combine the chicken, sweet chilli sauce and fish sauce in a bowl.
3 Heat a wok over high heat, add the oil and swirl to coat. Add the chicken pieces and stir-fry for 3–5 minutes, or until cooked through. Add the corn and sugar snap peas and stir-fry for 2 minutes. Add the noodles and lime juice and serve.

NUTRITION PER SERVE (6)
Protein 30 g; Fat 6.5 g; Carbohydrate 50 g; Dietary Fibre 4 g; Cholesterol 53 mg; 1593 kJ (380 cal)

NOTE: If thigh fillets are unavailable, use 3 breast fillets.

Soak the noodles in boiling water and separate them with a fork.

Mix together the chicken pieces, sweet chilli sauce and fish sauce.

Add the noodles and lime juice to the wok just before serving.

CHICKEN NASI GORENG

Preparation time: 25 minutes
Total cooking time: 15 minutes
Serves 4–6

- 5–8 long red chillies, seeded and chopped
- 2 teaspoons shrimp paste
- 8 cloves garlic, finely chopped
- oil, for cooking
- 2 eggs, lightly beaten
- 350 g (12 oz) chicken thigh fillets, cut into thin strips
- 200 g (6 1/2 oz) peeled raw prawns, deveined
- 8 cups (1.5 kg/3 lb) cooked rice
- 1/3 cup (80 ml/2 3/4 fl oz) kecap manis
- 1/3 cup (80 ml/2 3/4 fl oz) soy sauce
- 2 small Lebanese cucumbers, finely chopped
- 1 large tomato, finely chopped
- lime wedges, to serve

1 Mix the chilli, shrimp paste and garlic in a food processor until the mixture resembles a paste.

2 Heat the wok until very hot, add 1 tablespoon of the oil and swirl it around to coat the side. Add the beaten eggs and, using a wok chan or metal egg flip, push the egg up the edges of the wok to form a large omelette. Cook for 1 minute over medium heat, or until the egg is set, then flip it over and cook the other side for 1 minute. Remove from the wok and cool before slicing into strips.

3 Reheat the wok, add 1 tablespoon of the oil and stir-fry the chicken and half the chilli paste over high heat until the chicken is just cooked. Remove the chicken from the wok.

4 Reheat the wok, add 1 tablespoon of the oil and stir-fry the prawns and the remaining chilli paste until the prawns are cooked. Remove from the wok and set aside.

5 Reheat the wok, add 1 tablespoon of the oil and the cooked rice, and toss constantly over medium heat for 4–5 minutes, or until the rice is heated through. Add the kecap manis and soy sauce, and toss constantly until all of the rice is coated in the sauces. Return the chicken and prawns to the wok, and toss until heated through. Season well with freshly cracked pepper and salt. Transfer to a large deep serving bowl and top with the omelette strips, cucumber and tomato. Serve with the lime wedges.

NUTRITION PER SERVE (6)
Protein 30 g; Fat 10 g; Carbohydrate 70 g; Dietary Fibre 3.5 g; Cholesterol 140 mg; 2105 kJ (505 cal)

Remove the seeds from the chillies and finely chop the flesh.

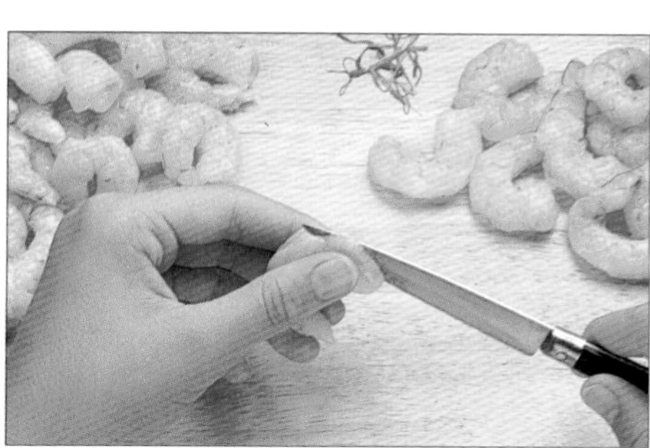

Slit the peeled prawns down the backs to remove the veins.

Process the chilli, shrimp paste and garlic until it forms a paste.

SPAGHETTI WITH OLIVE, CAPER AND ANCHOVY SAUCE

Preparation time: 15 minutes
Total cooking time: 20 minutes
Serves 6

375 g (12 oz) spaghetti
1/3 cup (80 ml/2 3/4 fl oz) olive oil
2 onions, finely chopped
3 cloves garlic, finely chopped
1/2 teaspoon chilli flakes
6 large ripe tomatoes, diced
4 tablespoons capers in brine, rinsed, drained
7–8 anchovies in oil, drained, minced
150 g (5 oz) Kalamata olives
3 tablespoons chopped fresh flat-leaf parsley

1 Cook the pasta in a large pan of rapidly boiling salted water until *al dente*. Drain and return to the pan to keep warm.

2 Meanwhile, heat the oil in a saucepan, add the onion and cook over medium heat for 5 minutes. Add the garlic and chilli flakes, and cook for 30 seconds, then add the tomato, capers and anchovies. Simmer over low heat for 5–10 minutes, or until thick and pulpy, then stir in the olives and parsley.

3 Stir the pasta through the sauce. Season and serve immediately with crusty bread.

NUTRITION PER SERVE
Protein 10 g; Fat 15 g; Carbohydrate 49 g; Dietary Fibre 6.5 g; Cholesterol 2 mg; 1563 kJ (373 cal)

The easiest way to mince the anchovies is with a mortar and pestle.

Cook the spaghetti in a pan of lightly salted boiling water until *al dente*.

Simmer the tomato and caper mixture over low heat until thick and pulpy.

PENNE WITH VEAL RAGOUT

Preparation time: 15 minutes
Total cooking time: 2 hours 40 minutes
Serves 4

2 onions, sliced
2 bay leaves, crushed
1.5 kg (3 lb) veal shin, cut into osso buco pieces (see NOTE)
1 cup (250 ml/8 fl oz) red wine
2 x 400 g (13 oz) cans crushed tomatoes
1 1/2 cups (375 ml/12 fl oz) beef stock
2 teaspoons chopped fresh rosemary
400 g (13 oz) penne
1 cup (150 g/5 oz) frozen peas

1 Preheat the oven to hot 220°C (425°F/Gas 7). Scatter the onion over the bottom of a large roasting tin, lightly spray with oil and place the bay leaves and veal pieces on top. Season with salt and pepper. Roast for 10–15 minutes, or until the veal is browned. Take care that the onion doesn't burn.

2 Pour the wine over the veal and return to the oven for a further 5 minutes. Reduce the heat to moderate 180°C (350°F/Gas 4), remove the tin from the oven and pour on the tomato, stock and 1 teaspoon of the rosemary. Cover with foil and return to the oven. Cook for 2 hours, or until the veal is starting to fall from the bone. Remove the foil and cook for a further 15 minutes, or until the meat loosens away from the bone and the liquid has evaporated slightly.

3 Cook the pasta in a large pan of rapidly boiling salted water until *al dente*. Drain and return to the pan to keep warm. Meanwhile, remove the veal from the oven and cool slightly. Add the peas and remaining rosemary and place over a hotplate. Cook over medium heat for 5 minutes, or until the peas are cooked. Serve the pasta topped with the ragout.

NUTRITION PER SERVE
Protein 52 g; Fat 5 g; Carbohydrate 81 g; Dietary Fibre 10 g; Cholesterol 125 mg; 2605 kJ (620 cal)

NOTE: Most butchers sell veal shin cut into osso buco pieces. If sold in a whole piece, ask the butcher to cut it for you (the pieces are about 3–4 cm thick). It is also available at some supermarkets. You can either remove the meat from the bone before serving, or leave it on.

Place the bay leaves and veal on top of the onion in the tin and roast until the veal is browned.

Cook the veal, covered and then uncovered, until it is falling away from the bone.

Add the frozen peas to the ragout and cook over medium heat for 5 minutes.

RED LENTIL PILAU

Preparation time: 15 minutes
Total cooking time: 25 minutes
Serves 4–6

GARAM MASALA
1 tablespoon coriander seeds
1 tablespoon cardamom pods
1 tablespoon cumin seeds
1 teaspoon whole black peppercorns
1 teaspoon whole cloves
1 small cinnamon stick, crushed

3 tablespoons oil
1 onion, chopped
3 cloves garlic, chopped
1 cup (200 g/6 1/2 oz) basmati rice
1 cup (250 g/8 oz) red lentils
3 cups (750 ml/24 fl oz) hot vegetable stock
spring onions, thinly sliced

1 To make the garam masala, place all the spices in a dry frying pan and shake over medium heat for 1 minute, or until fragrant. Blend in a spice grinder, blender or mortar and pestle to make a fine powder.
2 Heat the oil in a large saucepan. Add the onion, garlic and 3 teaspoons garam masala. Cook over medium heat for 3 minutes, or until soft.
3 Stir in the rice and lentils and cook for 2 minutes. Add the hot stock and stir well. Slowly bring to the boil, then reduce the heat and simmer, covered, for 15–20 minutes, or until the rice is cooked and all the stock has been absorbed. Gently fluff the rice with a fork. Garnish with spring onion.

NUTRITION PER SERVE (6)
Protein 13 g; Fat 11 g; Carbohydrate 42 g; Dietary Fibre 7 g; Cholesterol 0 mg; 1333 kJ (318 Cal)

NOTE: If time is short you can use ready-made garam masala instead of making your own.

Finely chop all the spices in a spice grinder until they make a fine powder.

Stir the rice and lentils into the onion and garlic mixture and cook for 2 minutes.

Simmer, covered, until the rice is cooked and all the stock has been absorbed.

JAPANESE FRIED PORK AND NOODLES

Preparation time: 30 minutes
Total cooking time: 15 minutes
Serves 4

1 tablespoon oil
150 g (5 oz) pork loin, thinly sliced
5 spring onions, cut into short lengths
1 carrot, cut into thin strips
200 g (6 1/2 oz) Chinese cabbage, shredded
500 g (1 lb) Hokkien noodles, gently pulled apart to separate
2 tablespoons shoshoyu
1 tablespoon Worcestershire sauce
1 tablespoon mirin
2 teaspoons caster sugar
1 cup (90 g/3 oz) bean sprouts, scraggly ends removed
1 sheet toasted nori, shredded

1 Heat the oil in a large wok over medium heat. Stir-fry the pork, spring onion and carrot for 1–2 minutes, or until the pork just changes colour.

2 Add the cabbage, noodles, shoshoyu, Worcestershire sauce, mirin, sugar and 2 tablespoons water. Cover and cook for 1 minute.

3 Add the bean sprouts and toss well to coat the vegetables and noodles in the sauce. Serve immediately, sprinkled with the shredded nori.

NUTRITION PER SERVE
Protein 25 g; Fat 8 g; Carbohydrate 93 g; Dietary Fibre 5.5 g; Cholesterol 40 mg; 2300 kJ (550 cal)

Finely shred the Chinese cabbage with a large, sharp knife.

Use your fingers to remove the scraggly ends from the bean sprouts.

Stir-fry the pork, spring onion and carrot until the pork just changes colour.

POTATO GNOCCHI WITH TOMATO-OLIVE SAUCE

Preparation time: 10 minutes
Total cooking time: 15 minutes
Serves 4

500 g (1 lb) fresh potato gnocchi
2 tablespoons oil
1 leek, sliced
1 cup (250 g/8 oz) bottled tomato pasta sauce
2/3 cup (170 ml/5 1/2 fl oz) vegetable stock
1/3 cup (60 g/2 oz) chopped black olives
6 anchovies, chopped

1 Cook the gnocchi in a large pan of rapidly boiling salted water until it floats to the surface. Lift out with a slotted spoon. Meanwhile, heat the oil in a large pan and add the leek. Stir over medium heat for 2 minutes or until tender. Add the tomato sauce, stock, olives and anchovies and stir for 5 minutes to heat through. Serve over the gnocchi.

NUTRITION PER SERVE
Protein 6 g; Fat 11 g; Carbohydrate 25 g; Dietary Fibre 5 g; Cholesterol 2 mg; 930 kJ (222 cal)

STORAGE: The sauce will keep for a day, covered, in the fridge.

NOTE: Fresh potato gnocchi is available from supermarkets and delicatessens. Use any other dried or fresh pasta if you prefer.

Add the tomato sauce, stock, olives and anchovies to the sauce and heat through.

PASTA WITH PEAS AND BABY ONIONS

Preparation time: 10 minutes
Total cooking time: 15–20 minutes
Serves 4–6

500 g (1 lb) spaghetti or vermicelli
2 bunches baby onions
1 tablespoon olive oil
4 rashers bacon, chopped
2 teaspoons plain flour
1 cup (250 ml/8 fl oz) light chicken or vegetable stock
1/2 cup (125 ml/4 fl oz) white wine
1 cup (150 g/5 oz) shelled fresh peas

1 Cook the pasta in a large pan of rapidly boiling salted water until *al dente*. Drain well and return to the pan to keep warm.
2 Meanwhile, trim the outer skins and ends from the baby onions, leaving only a small section of the green stem attached. Heat the oil in a large heavy-based deep pan. Add the bacon and the trimmed onions and stir over low heat for 4 minutes, or until golden. Sprinkle the flour lightly over the top and stir for 1 minute.
3 Combine the stock and wine and add to the pan. Increase the heat and bring to the boil. Add the peas and cook for 5 minutes, or until the onions and peas are just tender.
4 Grind black pepper onto the sauce, then toss gently with the pasta.

NUTRITION PER SERVE (6)
Protein 16 g; Fat 6 g; Carbohydrate 65 g; Dietary Fibre 7 g; Cholesterol 10 mg; 1635 kJ (390 cal)

NOTE: Fresh peas are authentic and have the best flavour for this recipe, but you can use frozen if fresh are not available.

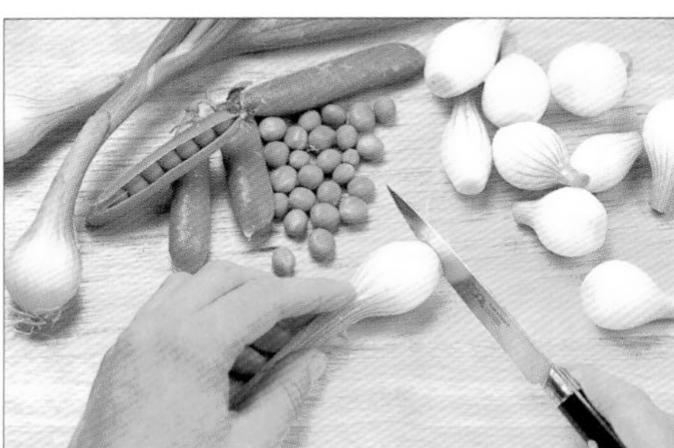

Trim the baby onions, leaving only a small section of green stem.

Add the onions and the bacon and stir over low heat until golden.

Combine the stock and wine and add to the onion and bacon mixture.

Grind black pepper, to taste, onto the cooked sauce in the pan.

THAI NOODLES WITH BEAN CURD

Preparation time: 25 minutes
+ 20 minutes soaking
Total cooking time: 5–7 minutes
Serves 4–6

- 8 dried Chinese mushrooms
- 250 g (8 oz) rice vermicelli
- 2 tablespoons oil
- 3 cloves garlic, chopped
- 5 cm (2 inch) piece fresh ginger, grated
- 100 g (3 1/2 oz) deep-fried tofu puffs, cut into small pieces
- 1 carrot, cut into matchsticks
- 100 g (3 1/2 oz) green beans, cut into short lengths
- 1/2 red capsicum, cut into matchsticks
- 2 tablespoons Golden Mountain sauce
- 1 tablespoon fish sauce
- 2 teaspoons soft brown sugar
- 100 g (3 1/2 oz) bean sprouts
- 1 cup (90 g/3 oz) finely shredded cabbage
- 60 g (2 oz) bean sprouts, extra, straggly ends removed, to garnish
- chilli sauce, for serving

1 Soak the dried Chinese mushrooms in hot water for 20 minutes. Drain and then slice.
2 In a heatproof bowl, pour boiling water over the vermicelli and soak for 1–4 minutes, or until soft. Drain.
3 Heat a wok, add the oil and, when very hot, add the garlic, ginger and tofu and stir-fry 1 minute. Add the carrot, beans, capsicum and mushrooms to the wok and stir-fry for 2 minutes. Add the sauces and sugar and toss well. Cover the wok and steam for 1 minute.
4 Add the vermicelli, bean sprouts and all but a few tablespoonsful of cabbage. Toss, cover and steam for 30 seconds. Arrange the noodles on a serving plate and garnish with the bean sprouts and remaining cabbage and serve with chilli sauce.

NUTRITION PER SERVE (6)
Protein 5 g; Fat 8.5 g; Carbohydrate 15 g; Dietary Fibre 5 g; Cholesterol 0 mg; 656 kJ (157 cal)

Cut the deep-fried tofu puffs into small cubes, using a sharp knife.

Place the vermicelli noodles in a heatproof bowl and pour boiling water over them.

Stir-fry the garlic, ginger and tofu in the hot oil for 1 minute.

Add the vermicelli, bean sprouts and cabbage to the wok, toss well and steam for 30 seconds.

PRAWNS WITH JASMINE RICE

Preparation time: 15 minutes
Total cooking time: 30 minutes
Serves 4

1 tablespoon peanut oil
8 spring onions, sliced
1 tablespoon finely chopped fresh ginger
1 tablespoon finely sliced lemon grass, white part only
2 teaspoons crushed coriander seeds (see NOTE)
2 cups (400 g/13 oz) jasmine rice
1 litre vegetable stock
1 tablespoon shredded lime rind
1 kg (2 lb) raw prawns, peeled, deveined and chopped
2 tablespoons lime juice
1 cup (30 g/1 oz) fresh coriander leaves
fish sauce, for serving

1 Heat the oil in a saucepan, add the spring onion and cook over low heat for 4 minutes, or until soft. Add the ginger, lemon grass, coriander seeds and rice, and stir for 1 minute.
2 Add the stock and lime rind and bring to the boil while stirring. Reduce the heat to very low and cook, covered, for 15–20 minutes, or until the rice is tender to the bite.
3 Remove the pan from the heat and stir in the prawns. Cover and leave for 4–5 minutes, or until the prawns are cooked. Add the lime juice and coriander leaves and fluff the rice with a fork. Sprinkle with a few drops of fish sauce to serve.

NUTRITION PER SERVE
Protein 59 g; Fat 12 g; Carbohydrate 80 g; Dietary Fibre 3 g; Cholesterol 373 mg; 2850 kJ (681 Cal)

NOTE: To crush coriander seeds, place in a small plastic bag and, using a rolling pin, crush until fine.

Peel and devein the prawns and chop them into small pieces.

Add the ginger, lemon grass, coriander seeds and rice to the saucepan.

Add the lime juice and coriander leaves and fluff the rice with a fork.

CHICKEN AND VEGETABLE LASAGNE

Preparation time: 45 minutes
Total cooking time: 1 hour 20 minutes
Serves 8

500 g (1 lb) chicken breast fillets
cooking oil spray
2 cloves garlic, crushed
1 onion, chopped
2 zucchini, chopped
2 celery stalks, chopped
2 carrots, chopped
300 g (10 oz) pumpkin, diced
2 x 400 g (13 oz) cans crushed tomatoes
2 sprigs fresh thyme
2 bay leaves
1/2 cup (125 ml/4 fl oz) white wine
2 tablespoons tomato paste
2 tablespoons chopped fresh basil
500 g (1 lb) English spinach
500 g (1 lb) cottage cheese
450 g (14 oz) ricotta
1/4 cup (60 ml/2 fl oz) skim milk
1/2 teaspoon ground nutmeg
1/3 cup (35 g/1 1/4 oz) grated Parmesan
300 g (10 oz) lasagne sheets

1 Preheat the oven to moderate 180°C (350°F/Gas 4). Trim any excess fat from the chicken breasts, then finely mince in a food processor. Heat a large, deep, non-stick frying pan, spray lightly with oil and cook the chicken mince in batches until browned. Remove and set aside.

2 Add the garlic and onion to the pan and cook until softened. Return the chicken to the pan and add the zucchini, celery, carrot, pumpkin, tomato, thyme, bay leaves, wine and tomato paste. Simmer, covered, for 20 minutes. Remove the bay leaves and thyme, stir in the fresh basil and set aside.

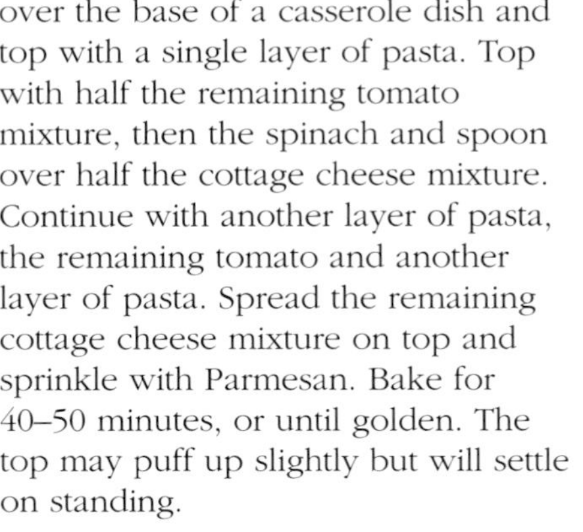

3 Shred the spinach and set aside. Mix the cottage cheese, ricotta, skim milk, nutmeg and half the Parmesan.

4 Spoon a little of the tomato mixture over the base of a casserole dish and top with a single layer of pasta. Top with half the remaining tomato mixture, then the spinach and spoon over half the cottage cheese mixture. Continue with another layer of pasta, the remaining tomato and another layer of pasta. Spread the remaining cottage cheese mixture on top and sprinkle with Parmesan. Bake for 40–50 minutes, or until golden. The top may puff up slightly but will settle on standing.

NUTRITION PER SERVE
Protein 40 g; Fat 10 g; Carbohydrate 35 g; Dietary Fibre 7 g; Cholesterol 70 mg; 1790 kJ (430 cal)

Finely mince the trimmed chicken fillets in a food processor.

Add the vegetables with the bay leaves, thyme, wine and tomato paste to the pan.

TAGLIATELLE WITH SWEET TOMATO AND WALNUT SAUCE

Preparation time: 20 minutes
Total cooking time: 45 minutes
Serves 4–6

4 ripe Roma tomatoes
1 tablespoon oil
1 onion, finely chopped
1 celery stalk, finely chopped
1 carrot, grated
2 tablespoons chopped fresh parsley
1 teaspoon red wine vinegar
1/4 cup (60 ml/2 fl oz) white wine
500 g (1 lb) tagliatelle or fettucine
1 tablespoon olive oil, extra
3/4 cup (90 g/3 oz) walnuts, roughly chopped
grated Parmesan, for serving

1 Score a cross on the bottom of each tomato, place in boiling water for 1 minute, then plunge into cold water. Peel the skin away from the cross and roughly chop the tomatoes.
2 Heat oil in a large heavy-based pan and cook the onion and celery for 5 minutes over low heat, stirring regularly. Add the tomatoes, carrot, parsley and combined vinegar and wine. Reduce the heat and simmer for 25 minutes. Season to taste.
3 Meanwhile, cook the pasta in a large pan of rapidly boiling salted water until *al dente*. Drain and return to the pan to keep warm.
4 Heat the extra oil in a frying pan and stir the walnuts over low heat for 5 minutes. Toss the pasta and sauce together and serve topped with walnuts and Parmesan cheese.

NUTRITION PER SERVE (6)
Protein 13 g; Fat 10 g; Carbohydrate 61 g; Dietary Fibre 6 g; Cholesterol 7 mg; 1654 kJ (395 Cal)

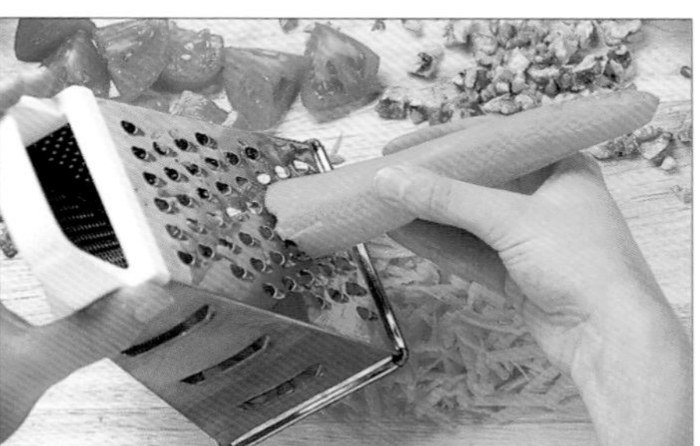

Peel the carrot if it needs it, before grating. Peel the tomatoes and roughly chop.

Cook the onion and celery before adding the tomatoes, carrot, parsley, vinegar and wine.

Gently fry the walnuts over low heat to bring out the flavour.

Toss together the pasta and sauce before serving topped with the walnuts.

RICE WITH CHICKEN AND SEAFOOD

Preparation time: 40 minutes
Total cooking time: 1 hour 10 minutes
Serves 4–6

- 500 g (1 lb) raw medium prawns
- 500 g (1 lb) mussels
- 200 g (6½ oz) calamari tubes
- ¼ cup (60 ml/2 fl oz) oil
- 2 chorizo sausages, thickly sliced
- 500 g (1 lb) chicken pieces
- 300 g (10 oz) pork fillet, thickly sliced
- 4 cloves garlic, crushed
- 2 red onions, chopped
- ¼ teaspoon saffron threads, soaked in hot water
- ¼ teaspoon turmeric
- 4 large tomatoes, peeled, seeded and chopped
- 2 cups (440 g/14 oz) short-grain rice
- 1.25 litres hot chicken stock
- 125 g (4 oz) green beans, cut into 4 cm (1½ inch) lengths
- 1 red capsicum, cut into thin strips
- 1 cup (155 g/5 oz) fresh peas

1 Peel the prawns. Devein, leaving the tails intact. Scrub the mussels and remove the beards. Cut the calamari tubes into 5 mm (¼ inch) thin slices. Heat 1 tablespoon of the oil in a large, heavy-based pan and add the chorizo. Cook over medium heat for 5 minutes, or until browned. Drain on paper towels. Add the chicken pieces and cook for 5 minutes, or until golden, turning once. Drain on paper towels.

2 Add the pork to the pan and cook for 3 minutes, or until browned, turning once. Drain on paper towels. Heat the remaining oil in the pan, add the garlic, onion, drained saffron and turmeric, and cook over medium heat for 3 minutes, or until the onion is soft. Add the tomato and cook for 3 minutes, or until soft.

3 Add the rice and stir for 5 minutes, or until the rice is translucent. Stir in the hot chicken stock, bring to the boil, cover and simmer for 10 minutes. Add the chicken, cover and cook for 20 minutes. Add the pork, prawns, mussels, calamari, chorizo and vegetables. Cover and cook for 10 minutes, or until the liquid has been absorbed.

NUTRITION PER SERVE (6)
Protein 66 g; Fat 12 g; Carbohydrate 66 g; Dietary Fibre 6 g; Cholesterol 278 mg; 2695 kJ (644 Cal)

Drain the cooked chorizo sausage slices on paper towels.

Cook the pork slices until they are browned on both sides.

Add the rice to the pan and stir until the rice is translucent.

casseroles, roasts & bakes

FILLET OF BEEF WITH MUSTARD COATING

Preparation time: 1 hour + 1 hour standing
Total cooking time: 40 minutes
Serves 8

2 kg (4 lb) scotch fillet of beef
3 tablespoons brandy
4 tablespoons wholegrain mustard
3 tablespoons cream
3/4 teaspoon coarsely ground black pepper

1 Prepare a covered barbecue for indirect cooking at moderate heat (normal fire), see page 7. Trim the meat of excess fat and sinew and tie securely with string at regular intervals to retain its shape. Brush all over with the brandy and leave for 1 hour.
2 Mix together the mustard, cream and pepper and spread evenly over the fillet.
3 Place the meat on a large greased sheet of foil. Pinch the corners securely to form a tray to hold in the juices. Cover the barbecue and cook for 30–40 minutes for medium-rare meat. Leave for 10–15 minutes before carving into thick slices. If you like, stir a tablespoon of mustard into the pan juices to make a gravy.

NUTRITION PER SERVE
Protein 54 g; Fat 14 g; Carbohydrate 0 g; Dietary Fibre 0 g; Cholesterol 130 mg; 1480 kJ (350 cal)

STORAGE: The beef can be marinated in brandy for up to a day. Keep, covered, in the fridge.

Tie the meat at intervals with string so that it keeps its shape.

Mix together the mustard, cream and pepper and spread over the meat.

Pinch up the corners of the foil to make a tray that will hold the meat juices.

CHICKEN PIES

Preparation time: 50 minutes + 30 minutes refrigeration
Total cooking time: 1 hour
Makes 4

300 g (10 oz) chicken breast fillet
1 bay leaf
2 cups (500 ml/16 oz) chicken stock
2 large potatoes, chopped
250 g (8 oz) orange sweet potato, chopped
2 celery sticks, chopped
2 carrots, chopped
1 onion, chopped
1 parsnip, chopped
1 clove garlic, crushed
1 tablespoon cornflour
1 cup (250 ml/8 fl oz) skim milk
1 cup (150 g/5 oz) frozen peas, thawed
1 tablespoon chopped chives
1 tablespoon chopped fresh parsley
1 1/2 cups (185 g/6 oz) self-raising flour
20 g (3/4 oz) butter
1/3 cup (80 ml/2 3/4 fl oz) milk
1 egg, lightly beaten
1/2 teaspoon sesame seeds

1 Put the chicken, bay leaf and stock in a large, deep frying pan and simmer over low heat for 10 minutes, until the chicken is cooked through. Lift out the chicken and cut into small pieces. Add the chopped potato, sweet potato, celery and carrot to the pan and simmer, covered, for 10 minutes, until just tender. Remove the vegetables from the pan with a slotted spoon.

2 Add the onion, parsnip and garlic to the pan and simmer, uncovered, for 10 minutes, or until very soft. Discard the bay leaf. Purée in a food processor until smooth.

3 Stir the cornflour into 2 tablespoons of the skim milk to make a smooth paste. Stir into the puréed mixture with the remaining milk and then return to the pan. Stir over low heat until the mixture boils and thickens. Preheat the oven to 200°C (400°F/Gas 6).

4 Combine the puréed mixture with the vegetables, chicken and herbs. Season and spoon into four 1 3/4 cup (440 ml/14 fl oz) ovenproof dishes.

5 To make the pastry, sift the flour into a large bowl, rub in the butter with your fingertips, then make a well in the centre. Combine the milk with 1/3 cup (80 ml/2 3/4 fl oz) water and add enough to the dry ingredients to make a soft dough. Turn out onto a lightly floured surface and knead until just smooth. Cut the dough into four portions and roll out to 1 cm (1/2 inch) larger than the tops of the dishes. Brush the edge of the dough with egg and fit over the top of each dish, pressing the edge firmly to seal.

6 Brush the pastry tops lightly with beaten egg and sprinkle with the sesame seeds. Bake for 30 minutes, until the pastry tops are golden.

NUTRITION PER PIE
Protein 30 g; Fat 10 g; Carbohydrate 65 g; Dietary Fibre 9.5 g; Cholesterol 100 mg; 2045 kJ (490 cal)

Purée the cooked onion, parsnip and garlic together until smooth.

Add enough liquid to the dry ingredients to make a soft dough.

Brush the edge of the pastry top with egg and then press over the pie dish.

BEEF BOURGUIGNON

Preparation time: 10 minutes
Total cooking time: 2 hours
Serves 6

1 kg (2 lb) topside or round steak
plain flour, seasoned with salt and pepper
3 rashers bacon, rind removed
1 tablespoon oil
12 pickling onions
1 cup (250 ml/ 8 fl oz) red wine
2 cups (500 ml/16 fl oz) beef stock
1 teaspoon dried thyme
200 g (6 1/2 oz) button mushrooms
2 bay leaves

1 Trim the steak of fat and sinew and cut into 2 cm (3/4 inch) cubes. Lightly toss in the seasoned flour to coat, shaking off the excess.
2 Cut the bacon into 2 cm (3/4 inch) squares. Heat the oil in a large pan and quickly cook the bacon over medium heat. Remove the bacon from the pan, then add the meat and brown well in batches. Remove and set aside. Add the onions to the pan and cook until golden.
3 Return the bacon and meat to the pan with the remaining ingredients. Bring to the boil, reduce the heat and simmer, covered, for 1 1/2 hours, or until the meat is very tender, stirring now and then. Remove the bay leaves to serve.

NUTRITION PER SERVE
Protein 40 g; Fat 7 g; Carbohydrate 5 g; Dietary Fibre 1 g; Cholesterol 90 mg; 1150 kJ (275 cal)

STORAGE TIME: Refrigerate in an airtight container for up to 3 days.

Trim the meat of any fat and sinew and cut it into cubes.

Return the bacon and meat to the pan and add the remaining ingredients.

BEEF, STOUT AND POTATO PIE

Preparation time: 30 minutes
Total cooking time: 3 hours 10 minutes
Serves 6

- 2 tablespoons olive oil
- 1.25 kg (2 lb 8 oz) chuck steak, cut into small cubes
- 2 onions, sliced
- 2 rashers bacon, roughly chopped
- 4 cloves garlic, crushed
- 2 tablespoons plain flour
- 440 ml (14 fl oz) can stout
- 1½ cups (375 ml/12 fl oz) beef stock
- 1½ tablespoons chopped fresh thyme
- 2 large potatoes, thinly sliced

1 Heat 1 tablespoon of the oil over high heat in a large flameproof casserole. Add the beef in batches and cook, stirring, for 5 minutes, or until the meat is browned. Remove from the dish. Reduce the heat to low, add the remaining oil, then cook the onion and bacon for 10 minutes, stirring occasionally. Add the garlic and cook for another minute. Return the beef to the casserole.

2 Sprinkle the flour over the beef, cook for a minute, stirring, and then gradually add the stout, stirring constantly. Add the stock, increase the heat to medium–high and bring to the boil. Stir in the thyme, season well, then reduce the heat and simmer for 2 hours, or until the beef is tender and the mixture has thickened.

3 Preheat the oven to 200°C (400°F/Gas 6). Lightly grease a 1.25 litre ovenproof dish and pour in the beef filling. Arrange potato slices in a single overlapping layer over the top to cover the meat. Brush lightly with olive oil and sprinkle with salt. Bake for 30–40 minutes, or until golden.

NUTRITION PER SERVE
Protein 49 g; Fat 13 g; Carbohydrate 14 g; Dietary Fibre 2 g; Cholesterol 146 mg; 1665 kJ (400 cal)

Gradually add the stout to the beef mixture, stirring constantly.

Arrange the potato slices in a single overlapping layer to cover the meat.

CHICKEN WITH BAKED EGGPLANT AND TOMATO

Preparation time: 30 minutes
Total cooking time: 1 hour 30 minutes
Serves 4

1 red capsicum
1 eggplant
3 tomatoes, cut into quarters
200 g (6½ oz) large button mushrooms, halved
1 onion, cut into thin wedges
cooking oil spray
1½ tablespoons tomato paste
½ cup (125 ml/4 fl oz) chicken stock
¼ cup (60 ml/2 fl oz) white wine
2 lean slices bacon
4 chicken breast fillets
4 small fresh rosemary sprigs

1 Preheat the oven to moderately hot 200°C (400°F/Gas 6). Cut the capsicum and eggplant into bite-sized pieces and combine with the tomato, mushrooms and onion in a baking dish. Spray with oil and bake for 1 hour, or until starting to brown and soften, stirring once.

2 Pour the combined tomato paste, stock and wine into the dish and bake for 10 minutes, or until thickened.

3 Meanwhile, discard the fat and rind from the bacon and cut in half. Wrap a strip of bacon around each chicken breast and secure it underneath with a toothpick. Poke a sprig of fresh rosemary underneath the bacon. Pan-fry in a lightly oiled, non-stick frying pan over medium heat until golden on both sides. Cover and cook for 10–15 minutes, or until the chicken is tender and cooked through. Remove the toothpicks. Serve the chicken on the vegetable mixture, surrounded with the sauce.

NUTRITION PER SERVE
Protein 35 g; Fat 4.5 g; Carbohydrate 8 g; Dietary Fibre 5 g; Cholesterol 70 mg; 965 kJ (230 cal)

Spray the vegetables lightly with the cooking oil before baking.

When the vegetables have softened, add the combined tomato paste, stock and wine.

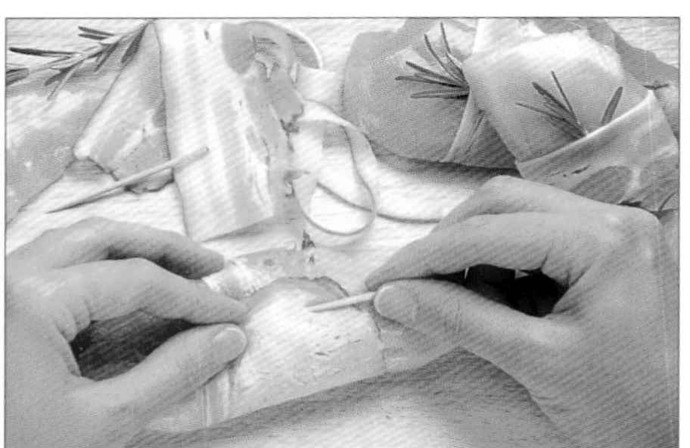

Wrap a strip of bacon around the chicken and secure underneath with a toothpick.

SMOKED SALMON PIZZAS

Preparation time: 20 minutes
Total cooking time: 15 minutes
Serves 6

250 g (8 oz) low-fat ricotta
6 small oval pitta breads
125 g (4 oz) sliced smoked salmon
1 small red onion, sliced
1 tablespoon baby capers
small dill sprigs, to garnish
1 lemon, cut into thin wedges, for serving

1 Preheat the oven to moderate 180°C (350°F/Gas 4). Put the ricotta in a bowl, season well with salt and pepper and stir until smooth. Spread the ricotta over the breads, leaving a clear border around the edge.
2 Top each pizza with some smoked salmon slices, then some onion pieces. Scatter baby capers over the top and bake on a baking tray for 15 minutes, or until the bases are slightly crispy around the edges. Garnish with a few dill sprigs and serve with lemon wedges.

NUTRITION PER SERVE
Protein 20 g; Fat 8 g; Carbohydrate 60 g; Dietary Fibre 4 g; Cholesterol 30 mg; 1650 kJ (395 Cal)

Peel the small red onion and then cut it into thin slices.

Spread the seasoned ricotta over the pitta breads, leaving a border around the edge.

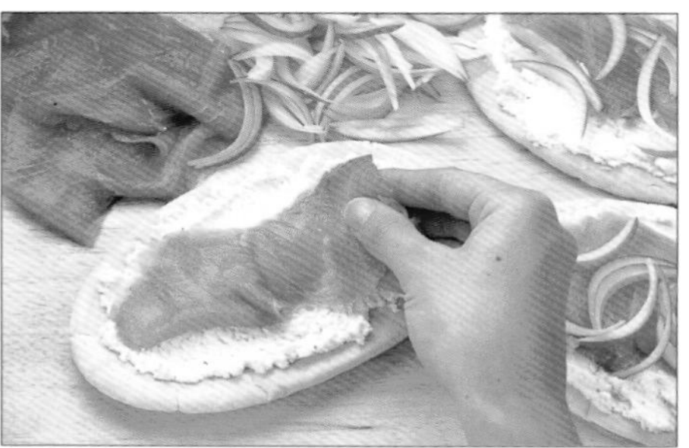

Put some smoked salmon slices over the ricotta, followed by onion and capers.

GARLIC ROAST CHICKEN

Preparation time: 10 minutes
Total cooking time: 1 hour
Serves 6

1.8 kg (3 lb 10 oz) chicken
1/2 teaspoon cracked peppercorns
1 whole head garlic
small bunch fresh oregano
3 tablespoons olive oil

1 Prepare a covered barbecue for indirect cooking at moderate heat (normal fire), see page 7. Place a drip tray under the top grill. Wipe the chicken and pat dry with paper towel. Season the cavity with salt and pepper. Using a sharp knife, cut the top off the head of garlic. Push the whole head of garlic, unpeeled, into the cavity. Follow with the whole bunch of oregano. Close the cavity with several toothpicks or a skewer.

2 Rub the chicken skin with salt and brush with oil. Place on the barbecue over the drip tray. Cover and cook for 1 hour, brushing occasionally with olive oil to keep the skin moist. Test the chicken by poking a skewer into the thigh—if the juices run clear the chicken is cooked through. Leave the chicken for 5 minutes before carving.

3 Carefully separate the garlic cloves and serve 1 or 2 cloves with each serving of chicken. (The soft flesh can be squeezed from the clove and eaten with the chicken.)

NUTRITION PER SERVE
Protein 21 g; Fat 14 g; Carbohydrate 0 g; Dietary Fibre 0 g; Cholesterol 70 mg; 875 kJ (210 cal)

STORAGE: The chicken can be kept warm in the barbecue with the top and bottom vents open.

HINT: Toast slices of French bread and spread with the soft, cooked garlic. Add a drizzle of olive oil and season with salt and pepper.

Cut the top off the head of garlic and then cook in the cavity of the chicken.

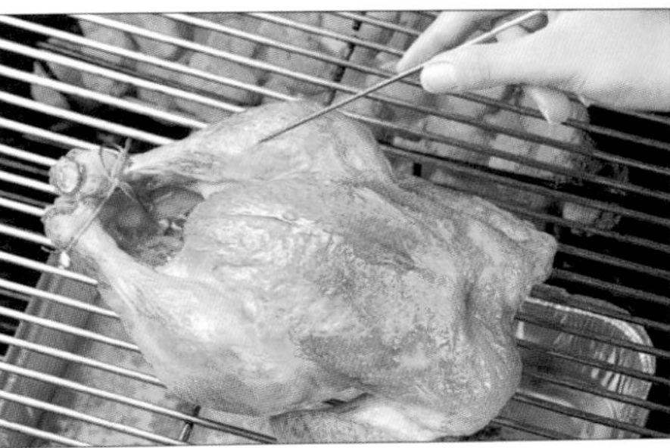

Test that the chicken is cooked by poking the thickest part of the thigh with a skewer.

Separate the cooked cloves of garlic and serve a couple with each portion of chicken.

OVEN-BAKED POTATO, LEEK AND OLIVES

Preparation time: 20 minutes
Total cooking time: 1 hour
Serves 4–6

2 tablespoons extra virgin olive oil
1 leek, finely sliced
1 1/2 cups (375 ml/12 fl oz) vegetable stock
2 teaspoons chopped fresh thyme
1 kg (2 lb) potatoes, unpeeled, cut into thin slices
6–8 pitted black olives, sliced
1/2 cup (60 g/2 oz) grated Parmesan
30 g (1 oz) butter, chopped

1 Preheat the oven to moderate 180°C (350°F/Gas 4). Brush a shallow 1.25 litre (40 fl oz) ovenproof dish with a little olive oil. Heat the remaining oil in a large pan and cook the leek over moderate heat until soft. Add the stock, thyme and potato. Cover and leave to simmer for 5 minutes.
2 Using tongs, lift out half the potato and put in the ovenproof dish. Sprinkle with olives and Parmesan and season with salt and pepper.
3 Layer with the remaining potato, then spoon the leek and stock mixture in at the side of the dish, keeping the top dry.
4 Scatter chopped butter over the potato and then bake, uncovered, for 50 minutes, or until cooked and golden brown. Leave in a warm place for about 10 minutes before serving.

NUTRITION PER SERVE (6)
Protein 7.5 g; Fat 13 g; Carbohydrate 23 g; Dietary Fibre 3 g; Cholesterol 20 mg; 1019 kJ (243 cal)

NOTE: Keeping the top layer of potato dry as you pour in the stock mixture will give the dish a crisp finish.

Cook the leek until soft, then add the stock, thyme and potato.

Lift out half the potato with tongs and put into an ovenproof dish.

Spoon the leek and stock mixture around the side, trying to keep the top dry.

Bake, uncovered, until the potatoes on top are golden brown.

CRUMBED FISH WITH WASABI CREAM

Preparation time: 25 minutes + 15 minutes refrigeration
Total cooking time: 20 minutes
Serves 4

3/4 cup (60 g/2 oz) fresh breadcrumbs
3/4 cup (25 g/3/4 oz) cornflakes
1 sheet nori, torn roughly
1/4 teaspoon paprika
4 x 150 g (5 oz) pieces firm white fish fillets
plain flour, for dusting
1 egg white
1 tablespoon skim milk
1 spring onion, thinly sliced

WASABI CREAM
1/2 cup (125 g/4 oz) low-fat natural yoghurt
1 teaspoon wasabi (see NOTE)
1 tablespoon low-fat mayonnaise
1 teaspoon lime juice

1 Preheat the oven to moderate 180°C (350°F/Gas 4). Combine the crumbs, cornflakes, nori and paprika in a food processor and process until the nori is finely chopped.
2 Dust the fish lightly with plain flour, dip into the combined egg white and milk, then into the breadcrumb mixture. Press the crumb mixture on firmly, then refrigerate for 15 minutes.
3 Line a baking tray with non-stick baking paper and put the fish on the paper. Bake for 15–20 minutes, or until the fish flakes easily with a fork.
4 To make the wasabi cream, mix the ingredients thoroughly in a bowl. Serve with the fish and sprinkle with a little spring onion.

NUTRITION PER SERVE
Protein 35 g; Fat 6 g; Carbohydrate 25 g; Dietary Fibre 1 g; Cholesterol 105 mg; 1270 kJ (305 Cal)

NOTE: Wasabi paste and nori are both available from Japanese food stores.

Process the breadcrumbs, cornflakes, nori and paprika together.

Dust the fish with flour, dip in the egg and milk, then press in the breadcrumbs.

Thoroughly mix the wasabi cream ingredients in a bowl and then serve with the fish.

MOUSSAKA

Preparation time: 30 minutes
Total cooking time: 1 hour 30 minutes
Serves 6

1 kg (2 lb) eggplants
cooking oil spray
400 g (13 oz) lean lamb mince
2 onions, finely chopped
2 cloves garlic, crushed
400 g (13 oz) can tomatoes
1 tablespoon chopped fresh thyme
1 teaspoon chopped fresh oregano
1 tablespoon tomato paste
1/3 cup (80 ml/2 3/4 fl oz) dry white wine
1 bay leaf
1 teaspoon sugar

CHEESE SAUCE
1 1/4 cups (315 ml/10 fl oz) skim milk
2 tablespoons plain flour
1/4 cup (30 g/1 oz) grated reduced-fat Cheddar
1 cup (250 g/8 oz) ricotta
pinch of cayenne pepper
1/4 teaspoon ground nutmeg

1 Cut the eggplant into 1 cm (1/2 inch) thick slices, place in a colander over a large bowl, layering with a generous sprinkling of salt, and leave to stand for 20 minutes. This is to draw out the bitter juices.
2 Lightly spray a non-stick frying pan with oil and brown the lamb mince, in batches if necessary, over medium-high heat. Once all the meat is browned, set aside.
3 Spray the pan again with oil, add the onion and stir continuously for 2 minutes. Add 1 tablespoon water to the pan to prevent sticking. Add the garlic and cook for about 3 minutes, or until the onion is golden brown.
4 Push the undrained tomatoes through a sieve, then discard the contents of the sieve.
5 Return the meat to the pan with the onion. Add the herbs, tomato pulp, tomato paste, wine, bay leaf and sugar. Cover and simmer over low heat for 20 minutes. Preheat a grill.
6 Thoroughly rinse and pat dry the eggplant, place on a grill tray, spray lightly with oil and grill under high heat until golden brown. Turn over, spray lightly with oil and grill until golden brown. Arrange half the eggplant slices over the base of a 1.5 litre capacity baking dish. Top with half the meat mixture and then repeat the layers.
7 Preheat the oven to moderate 180°C (350°F/Gas 4). To make the cheese sauce, blend a little of the milk with the flour to form a paste in a small pan. Gradually blend in the remaining milk, stirring constantly over low heat until the milk starts to simmer and thicken. Remove from the heat and stir in the Cheddar, ricotta, cayenne and nutmeg. Pour over the moussaka and bake for 35–40 minutes, or until the cheese is golden brown and the moussaka heated through.

NUTRITION PER SERVE
Protein 10 g; Fat 10 g; Carbohydrate 15 g; Dietary Fibre 5.5 g; Cholesterol 25 mg; 735 kJ (175 cal)

STORAGE TIME: Freeze for up to 2 months. Thaw in the fridge, then heat in a moderate oven for 30–45 minutes.

Sprinkle a generous amount of salt on the eggplant slices and set aside.

Empty the can of tomatoes into a sieve and push the tomatoes through.

Stir the herbs, tomato pulp, tomato paste, wine, bay leaf and sugar into the meat.

Rinse and dry the eggplant slices and grill on both sides until golden.

Layer the eggplant slices and meat evenly in the baking dish.

Remove from the heat before adding the Cheddar, ricotta, cayenne and nutmeg.

THAI-STYLE WHOLE SNAPPER

Preparation time: 10 minutes
Total cooking time: 30 minutes
Serves 6

2 garlic cloves, crushed
1 tablespoon fish sauce
2 tablespoons lemon juice
1 tablespoon grated fresh ginger
2 tablespoons sweet chilli sauce
1 tablespoon rice wine vinegar
2 tablespoons chopped fresh coriander
2 tablespoons white wine
600 g (1 1/4 lb) whole snapper, cleaned and scaled (ask your fishmonger to do this)
2 spring onions, cut into thin strips

1 Preheat the oven to moderately hot 190°C (375°F/ Gas 5). Place the crushed garlic, fish sauce, lemon juice, grated ginger, sweet chilli sauce, rice wine vinegar, coriander and wine in a small jug and mix together well.

2 Place the snapper on a large piece of foil on a baking tray. Pour the marinade over the fish and sprinkle with the spring onion.

3 Wrap some foil around the fish like a parcel and place in the oven. Bake for 20–30 minutes or until the flesh flakes easily when tested with a fork. Serve immediately with steamed rice.

NUTRITION PER SERVE

Protein 20 g; Fat 2 g; Carbohydrate 5 g; Dietary Fibre 0 g; Cholesterol 60 mg; 495 kJ (120 Cal)

Put the ingredients for the marinade in a jug and mix together well.

Pour the marinade over the snapper after you have placed it on the aluminium foil.

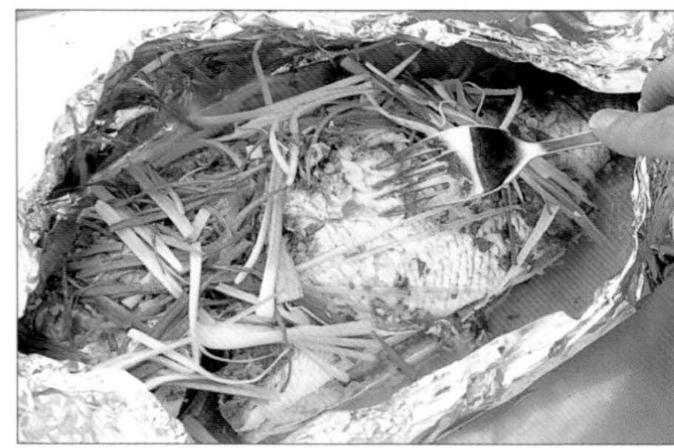

Cook the fish until the flesh flakes easily when tested with a fork.

SPINACH PIE

Preparation time: 25 minutes
Total cooking time: 45 minutes
Serves 6

1.5 kg (3 lb) English spinach
2 teaspoons olive oil
1 onion, chopped
4 spring onions, chopped
750 g (1 1/2 lb) reduced-fat cottage cheese
2 eggs, lightly beaten
2 cloves garlic, crushed
pinch of ground nutmeg
1/4 cup (15 g/1/2 oz) chopped fresh mint
8 sheets filo pastry
30 g (1 oz) butter, melted
1/2 cup (40 g/1 1/4 oz) fresh breadcrumbs

1 Preheat the oven to 180°C (350°F/ Gas 4). Lightly spray a square 1.5 litre capacity ovenproof dish with oil. Trim and wash the spinach, then place in a large pan with the water clinging to the leaves. Cover and cook for 2–3 minutes, until just wilted. Drain, cool then squeeze dry and chop.
2 Heat the oil in a small pan. Add the onion and spring onion and cook for 2–3 minutes, until softened. Combine in a bowl with the chopped spinach. Stir in the cottage cheese, egg, garlic, nutmeg and mint. Season and mix thoroughly.
3 Brush a sheet of filo pastry with a little butter. Fold in half widthways and line the base and sides of the dish. Repeat with 3 more sheets. Keep the unused sheets moist by covering with a damp tea towel.
4 Sprinkle the breadcrumbs over the pastry. Spread the filling into the dish. Fold over any overlapping pastry. Brush and fold another sheet and place on top. Repeat with 3 more sheets. Tuck the pastry in at the sides. Brush the top with any remaining butter. Score squares or diamonds on top using a sharp knife. Bake for 40 minutes, or until golden. Cut into squares to serve.

NUTRITION PER SERVE
Protein 35 g; Fat 10 g; Carbohydrate 30 g; Dietary Fibre 8 g; Cholesterol 75 mg; 1500 kJ (360 cal)

Squeeze any excess moisture out of the cooled spinach with your hands.

Line the base and sides of the dish with the greased and folded filo.

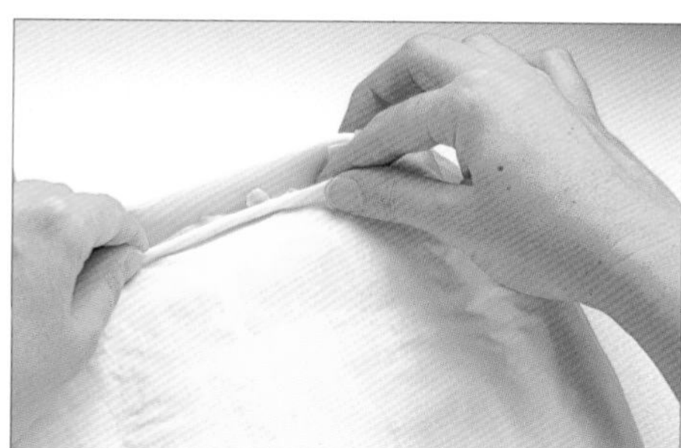

When you have lined the top with pastry, tuck it in at the sides.

ROSEMARY-INFUSED LAMB AND LENTIL CASSEROLE

Preparation time: 20 minutes
Total cooking time: 2 hours 30 minutes
Serves 6

1 tablespoon olive oil
1 onion, finely sliced
2 cloves garlic, crushed
1 small carrot, finely chopped
2 teaspoons cumin seeds
1/4 teaspoon chilli flakes
2 teaspoons finely chopped fresh ginger
1 kg (2 lb) boned leg of lamb, cut into 4 cm (1 1/2 inch) cubes
2 teaspoons fresh rosemary leaves, chopped
3 cups (750 ml/24 fl oz) chicken stock
1 cup (185 g/6 oz) green or brown lentils
3 teaspoons soft brown sugar
2 teaspoons balsamic vinegar

1 Preheat the oven to moderate 180°C (350°F/Gas 4). Heat half the oil in a large, heavy-based pan. Add the onion, garlic and carrot and cook over medium heat for about 5 minutes, or until soft and golden. Add the cumin seeds, chilli flakes and ginger, cook for 1 minute, then transfer to a large casserole dish.

2 Heat the remaining oil in the pan and brown the lamb in batches over high heat. Transfer to the casserole.

3 Add the rosemary to the pan and stir in 2 1/2 cups (625 ml/20 fl oz) of the stock. Heat until the stock is bubbling, then pour into the casserole dish. Cover the dish and bake in the oven for 1 hour.

4 Add the lentils, sugar and vinegar and cook for 1 hour more, or until the lentils are cooked. If the mixture is too thick, stir in the remaining stock. Season with salt and pepper to taste and serve.

NUTRITION PER SERVE
Protein 45 g; Fat 15 g; Carbohydrate 15 g; Dietary Fibre 5 g; Cholesterol 120 mg; 1618 kJ (385 cal)

When the oil is hot, add the onion, garlic and carrot and cook until soft and golden.

After browning the lamb, add the rosemary and stock to the pan.

Bake the casserole for 1 hour, then add the lentils, sugar and vinegar.

ORANGE ROASTED CHICKENS

Preparation time: 15 minutes + overnight marinating
Total cooking time: 40 minutes
Serves 8

2 x 800 g (1 lb 10 oz) chickens
100 g ($3^{1}/_{2}$ oz) butter, softened
2 cloves garlic, crushed
1 tablespoon finely grated orange rind
$^{1}/_{2}$ cup (60 ml/2 fl oz) orange juice

1 Preheat the oven to hot 220°C (425°F/Gas 7). Using kitchen scissors, cut the chickens in half through the backbone and breastbone. Pat dry with paper towels and wipe the inside.
2 Combine the butter, garlic and orange rind and beat well. Gently loosen the skin of the chickens by sliding your fingers between the flesh and the skin. Push the orange butter under the skin as evenly as possible. Put the chickens in a ceramic dish and pour the orange juice over them. Cover and refrigerate for 3 hours, or preferably overnight.
3 Drain the chicken pieces well and arrange cut-side down on roasting racks inside two baking dishes. Pour 2 tablespoons of water into each baking dish.
4 Roast for 30–40 minutes, or until the chickens are golden brown. Cover with foil and allow to rest for 15 minutes. Cut into quarters to serve.

NUTRITION PER SERVE
Protein 30 g; Fat 15 g; Carbohydrate 1 g; Dietary Fibre 0 g; Cholesterol 95 mg; 990 kJ (235 Cal)

NOTE: If you can, use freshly squeezed orange juice.

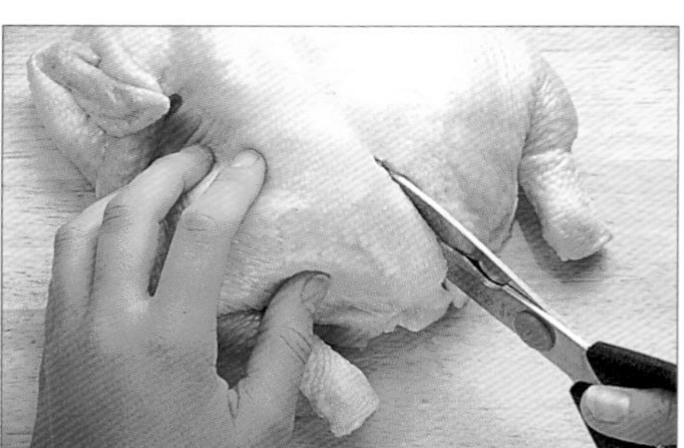

Cut the chickens in half through the backbone and breastbone.

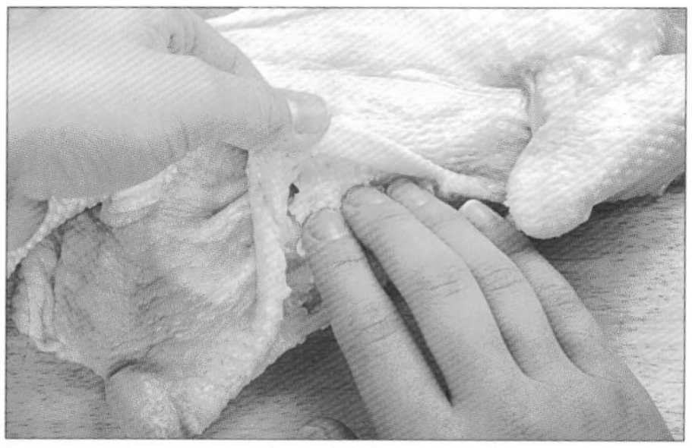

Loosen the skin of the chickens and spread the orange butter underneath.

Put the chicken pieces cut-side down on roasting racks inside the baking dishes.

desserts

BERRIES IN CHAMPAGNE JELLY

Preparation time: 10 minutes + refrigeration
Total cooking time: 5 minutes
Serves 8

1 litre champagne or sparkling wine
1 1/2 tablespoons gelatine
1 cup (250 g/8 oz) sugar
4 strips lemon rind
4 strips orange rind
1 2/3 cups (250 g/8 oz) small strawberries, hulled
1 2/3 cups (250 g/8 oz) blueberries

1 Pour 2 cups (500 ml/16 fl oz) champagne or sparkling white wine into a bowl and let the bubbles subside. Sprinkle the gelatine over the top in an even layer. Leave until the gelatine is spongy—do not stir. Place the remaining champagne in a large pan with the sugar, lemon and orange rind and heat gently, stirring, until all the sugar has dissolved.

2 Remove the pan from the heat, add the gelatine mixture and stir until thoroughly dissolved. Leave the jelly to cool completely, then remove the lemon and orange rind.

3 Divide the strawberries and blueberries among eight 1/2 cup (125 ml/4 fl oz) glasses or bowls and pour the jelly over them. Chill until the jelly has fully set. Remove from the fridge 15 minutes before serving.

NUTRITION PER SERVE

Protein 3 g; Fat 0 g; Carbohydrate 37 g; Dietary Fibre 1.5 g; Cholesterol 0 mg; 965 kJ (230 Cal)

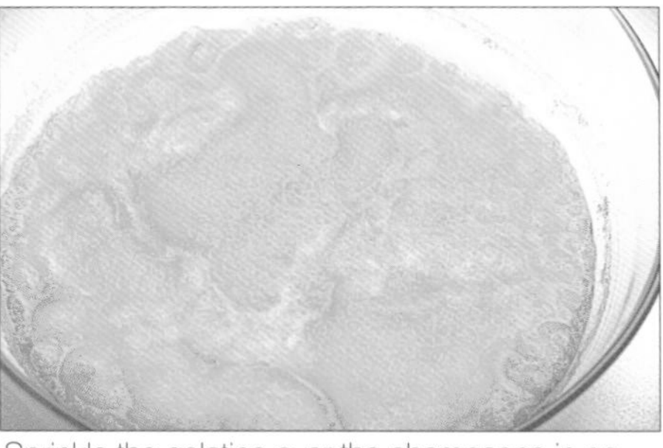

Sprinkle the gelatine over the champagne in an even layer and leave until spongy.

Pour the jelly into the wine glasses or bowls, covering the berries.

BAKED APPLES

Preparation time: 30 minutes
Total cooking time: 50 minutes
Serves 4

- 4 Granny Smith apples
- 50 g (1 3/4 oz) dried apricots, finely chopped
- 50 g (1 3/4 oz) dates, finely chopped
- 1 tablespoon dry breadcrumbs
- 1/2 teaspoon ground cinnamon
- 1 tablespoon honey, warmed
- 2 teaspoons apricot jam, warmed
- 20 g (3/4 oz) firm butter
- ground nutmeg, to serve

1 Preheat the oven to moderate 180°C (350°F/Gas 4) and lightly grease an ovenproof dish.
2 Core the apples and, using a small sharp knife, run a small slit around the circumference of each apple (this will stop it splitting during baking).
3 Combine the dried apricots, dates, breadcrumbs, cinnamon, honey and jam in a bowl. Divide the mixture into four, and push it into the apples using two teaspoons or your fingers. Dot the top of each apple with the butter, and put the apples in the prepared dish.
4 Bake for about 45–50 minutes, or until the apples are tender all the way through—test with a skewer to be absolutely sure. Serve hot with cream or ice cream. Sprinkle some nutmeg over the top before serving.

NUTRITION PER SERVE
Protein 1 g; Fat 4 g; Carbohydrate 30 g; Dietary Fibre 4 g; Cholesterol 13 mg; 685 kJ (165 Cal)

Carefully run a sharp knife around the circumference of each apple.

Push the mixture into each of the apples with teaspoons or your fingers.

POACHED PEARS IN SAFFRON CITRUS SYRUP

Preparation time: 10 minutes
Total cooking time: 30 minutes
Serves 4

- 1 vanilla bean, split lengthways
- 1/2 teaspoon firmly packed saffron threads
- 3/4 cup (185 g/6 oz) caster sugar
- 2 teaspoons grated lemon rind
- 4 firm, ripe pears, peeled
- biscotti, to serve (see NOTE)

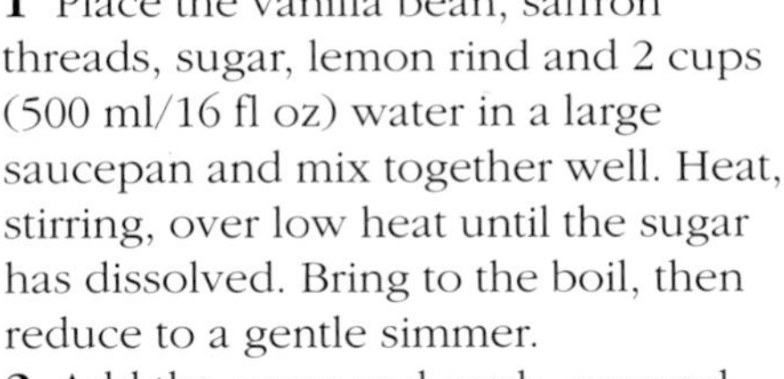

1 Place the vanilla bean, saffron threads, sugar, lemon rind and 2 cups (500 ml/16 fl oz) water in a large saucepan and mix together well. Heat, stirring, over low heat until the sugar has dissolved. Bring to the boil, then reduce to a gentle simmer.
2 Add the pears and cook, covered, for 12–15 minutes, or until tender when tested with a metal skewer. Turn the pears over with a slotted spoon halfway through cooking. Once cooked, remove from the syrup with a slotted spoon.
3 Remove the lid and allow the saffron citrus syrup to come to the boil. Cook for 8–10 minutes, or until the syrup has reduced by half and thickened slightly. Remove the vanilla bean and drizzle the syrup over the pears. Serve with biscotti.

NUTRITION PER SERVE
Protein 0.5 g; Fat 0 g; Carbohydrate 70 g; Dietary Fibre 4.5 g; Cholesterol 0 mg; 1155 kJ (276 Cal)

NOTE: Biscotti are available in a wide variety of flavours. You can buy biscotti at gourmet food stores, delicatessens and supermarkets.

Stir the saffron citrus syrup until the sugar has completely dissolved.

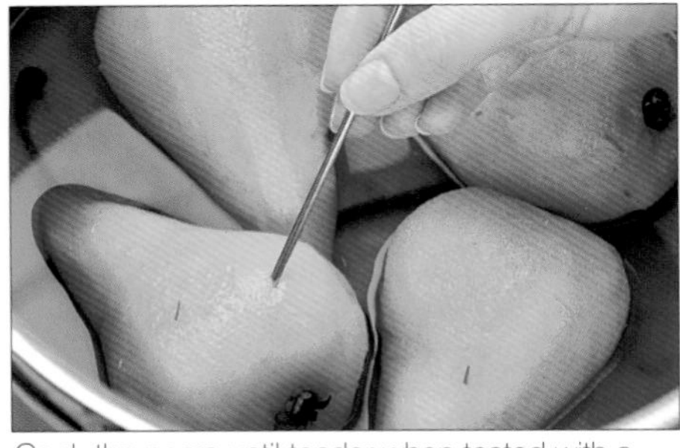

Cook the pears until tender when tested with a metal skewer.

Bring the syrup to the boil and cook until it has slightly thickened.

MANGO AND PASSIONFRUIT SORBET

Preparation time: 20 minutes + 8 hours freezing
Total cooking time: 5 minutes
Serves 6

1 cup (250 g/8 oz) caster sugar
1/3 cup (90 g/3 oz) passionfruit pulp
1/2 large mango (200 g/6 1/2 oz), chopped
1 large (250 g/8 oz) peach, chopped
2 tablespoons lemon juice
1 egg white

1 Stir the sugar in a pan with 1 cup (250 ml/8 fl oz) water over low heat until dissolved. Increase the heat, bring to the boil and boil for 1 minute. Transfer to a glass bowl, cool, then refrigerate. Strain the passionfruit pulp, reserving 1 tablespoon of the seeds.
2 Blend the fruit, passionfruit juice and lemon juice in a blender until smooth. With the motor running, add the cold sugar syrup and 150 ml (5 fl oz) water. Stir in the passionfruit seeds. Freeze in a shallow container, stirring occasionally, for about 5 hours, or until almost set.
3 Break up the icy mixture roughly with a fork or spoon, transfer to a bowl and beat with electric beaters until smooth and fluffy. Beat the egg white in a small bowl until firm peaks form, then fold into the mixture until just combined. Spread into a loaf tin and return to the freezer until firm. Transfer to the refrigerator, to soften, 15 minutes before serving.

NUTRITION PER SERVE
Protein 2 g; Fat 0 g; Carbohydrate 50 g; Dietary Fibre 3 g; Cholesterol 0 mg; 850 kJ (200 Cal)

VARIATION: To make a berry sorbet, use 200 g (6 1/2 oz) blackberries or blueberries, 200 g (6 1/2 oz) hulled strawberries and 50 g (1 3/4 oz) peach flesh. Prepare as above.

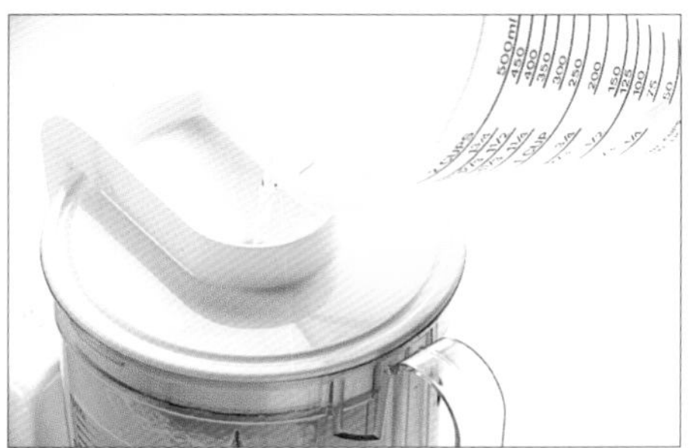

Leave the motor running and pour in the cold sugar syrup and water.

Gently fold the egg white into the smooth fruit purée with a metal spoon.

CARAMEL BANANAS

Preparation time: 5 minutes
Total cooking time: 10 minutes
Serves 4

60 g (2 oz) butter
100 g ($3^1/_2$ oz) soft brown sugar
2 tablespoons lemon juice
1 tablespoon orange liqueur
4 firm, ripe bananas, sliced in half lengthways

1 Melt the butter in a large frying pan. Add the sugar and stir to combine, then simmer for 3 minutes, or until golden and bubbly.
2 Add the lemon juice and liqueur, and stir gently. Put the bananas in the sauce and simmer for 5 minutes, or until the sauce thickens. Occasionally spoon the sauce over the bananas to baste them. The caramel bananas are delicious served with good-quality vanilla ice cream or with waffles and whipped cream.

NUTRITION PER SERVE
Protein 0 g; Fat 10 g; Carbohydrate 28 g; Dietary Fibre 0 g; Cholesterol 38 mg; 950 kJ (225 Cal)

VARIATION: This recipe also makes a delicious pancake filling if you chop the bananas instead of halving them.

Try stacking the pancakes between layers of bananas and sauce. Sprinkle over demerara sugar and flash under a grill until toffee-like.

Add the brown sugar to the pan when the butter has melted.

Put the bananas in the pan when the caramel is golden and bubbly.

Spoon the caramel sauce over the bananas to baste them.

RHUBARB AND PEAR CRUMBLE

Preparation time: 20 minutes
Total cooking time: 25 minutes
Serves 6

600 g (1 1/4 lb) rhubarb
2 strips lemon rind
1 tablespoon honey, or to taste
2 firm, ripe pears
1/4 cup (35 g/1 1/4 oz) wholemeal plain flour
1/2 cup (50 g/1 3/4 oz) rolled oats
1/3 cup (60 g/2 oz) soft brown sugar
50 g (1 3/4 oz) butter

1 Trim the rhubarb, wash and cut into 3 cm (1 1/4 inch) pieces. Place in a medium pan with the lemon rind and 1 tablespoon water. Cook, covered, over low heat for 10 minutes, or until tender. Cool a little. Stir in the honey and remove the lemon rind.

2 Preheat the oven to moderate 180°C (350°F/Gas 4). Peel, core and cut the pears into 2 cm (3/4 inch) cubes and combine with the rhubarb. Pour into a 1.25 litre dish and smooth the surface.

3 To make the topping, combine the flour, oats and brown sugar in a bowl. Rub in the butter with your fingertips until the mixture is crumbly. Spread over the fruit. Bake for 15 minutes, or until cooked and golden.

NUTRITION PER SERVE
Protein 3.5 g; Fat 8 g; Carbohydrate 30 g; Dietary Fibre 6 g; Cholesterol 0 mg; 885 kJ (210 Cal)

Trim the rhubarb, wash thoroughly, then cut into short pieces.

Add the cubed pears to the cooked rhubarb and gently stir to combine.

Use your fingertips to rub the butter into the dry ingredients to make a crumble topping.

LEMON GRASS AND GINGER INFUSED FRUIT SALAD

Preparation time: 20 minutes
Total cooking time: 10 minutes
Serves 4

1/4 cup (60 g/2 oz) caster sugar
2.5 cm x 2.5 cm (1 inch x 1 inch piece fresh ginger, thinly sliced
1 stem lemon grass, bruised and halved
1 large passionfruit
1 Fiji red pawpaw (560 g/14 oz)
1/2 honeydew melon (800 g/1 lb 10 oz)
1 large mango (500 g/1 lb)
1 small fresh pineapple (1 kg/2 lb)
12 fresh lychees
3 tablespoons shredded fresh mint

1 Place the sugar, ginger and lemon grass in a small saucepan, add 1/2 cup (125 ml/4 fl oz) water and stir over low heat to dissolve the sugar. Boil for 5 minutes, or until reduced to 1/3 cup (80 ml/2 3/4 fl oz) and cool. Strain the syrup and add the passionfruit pulp.
2 Peel and seed the pawpaw and melon. Cut into 4 cm cubes. Peel the mango and cut the flesh into cubes, discarding the stone. Peel, halve and core the pineapple and cut into cubes. Peel the lychees, then make a slit in the flesh and remove the seed.
3 Place all the fruit in a large serving bowl. Pour on the syrup, or serve separately if preferred. Garnish with the shredded mint.

NUTRITION PER SERVE
Protein 7 g; Fat 2 g; Carbohydrate 80 g; Dietary Fibre 13.5 g; Cholesterol 0 mg; 1485 kJ (355 Cal)

NOTE: If fresh lychees are not available, canned ones are fine.

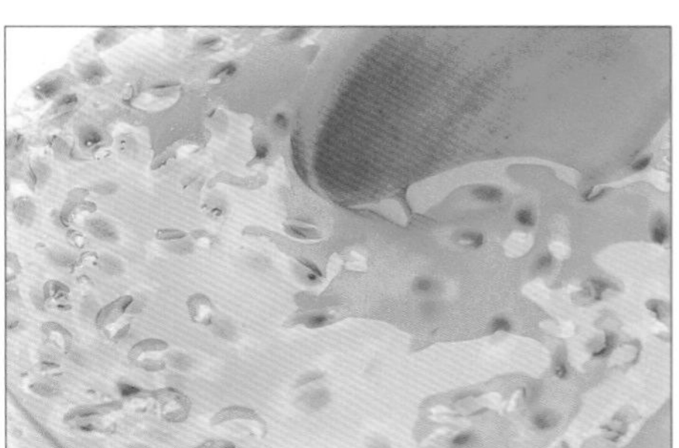

Stir the passionfruit pulp into the strained ginger and lemon grass syrup.

Peel the pawpaw, then remove the seeds with a spoon.

Peel the lychees, make a slit in the flesh and remove the seed.

POACHED DRIED FRUIT WITH WHOLE SPICES

Preparation time: 10 minutes + 2 hours soaking
Total cooking time: 30 minutes
Serves 8

- 1 orange
- 1 lemon
- 1 cup (250 ml/8 fl oz) apple juice
- 6 whole cardamom pods, lightly crushed
- 6 whole cloves
- 1 cinnamon stick
- 1/2 vanilla bean
- 375 g (12 oz) packet dried fruit salad
- 1/2 cup (125 g/4 oz) sugar
- 3 tablespoons soft brown sugar
- 1 tablespoon brandy

1 Peel 3 large strips of orange rind, avoiding too much white pith. Peel the lemon rind into thick strips. Cut half the rind into thin strips.
2 Put the apple juice, whole spices and thick strips of rind in a large pan with 3 cups (750 ml/24 fl oz) water and bring to the boil. Add the dried fruit. Remove from the heat and set aside for 2 hours.
3 Return to the heat, add the combined sugars and thin strips of rind and cover. Cook over low heat for 5 minutes, or until soft. Remove the fruit with a slotted spoon. Simmer the juice for another 5 minutes, or until reduced and thickened slightly. Add the brandy. Serve the fruit warm or cold, drizzled with juice.

NUTRITION PER SERVE
Protein 1 g; Fat 0.5 g; Carbohydrate 58 g; Dietary Fibre 3 g; Cholesterol 0 mg; 994 kJ (237 cal)

STORAGE: This will keep well for at least a week.

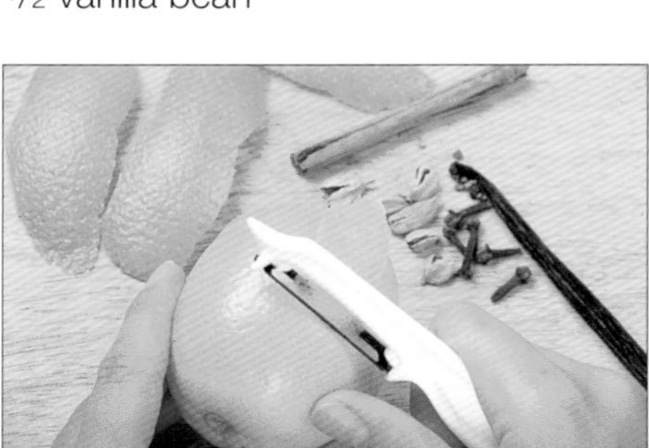

Use a vegetable peeler to remove 3 strips of the orange rind.

Put the apple juice, whole spices and thick strips of rind in a pan with water.

Remove the dried fruit from the poaching syrup with a slotted spoon.

WATERMELON AND VODKA GRANITA

Preparation time: 10 minutes + 5 hours freezing
Total cooking time: Nil
Serves 6

- 1 kg (2 lb) piece of watermelon, rind removed (to leave 600 g/1 1/4 lb flesh)
- 2 teaspoons lime juice
- 1/4 cup (60 g/2 oz) caster sugar
- 1/4 cup (60 ml/2 fl oz) citrus-flavoured vodka

1 Coarsely chop the watermelon, removing the seeds. Place the flesh in a food processor and add the lime juice and sugar. Process until smooth, then strain through a fine sieve. Stir in the vodka, then taste—if the watermelon is not very sweet, you may have to add a little more sugar.

2 Pour into a shallow 1.5 litre metal tin and freeze for about 1 hour, or until beginning to freeze around the edges. Scrape the frozen parts back into the mixture with a fork. Repeat every 30 minutes for about 4 hours, or until even ice crystals have formed.

3 Serve immediately or beat with a fork just before serving. To serve, scrape into dishes with a fork.

NUTRITION PER SERVE
Protein 0.5 g; Fat 0 g; Carbohydrate 18 g; Dietary Fibre 1 g; Cholesterol 0 mg; 410 kJ (98 Cal)

SERVING SUGGESTION: A scoop of the granita in a shot glass with vodka is great for summer cocktail parties.

VARIATION: A tablespoon of finely chopped mint may be stirred through the mixture after straining the liquid.

Coarsely chop the watermelon flesh, removing the seeds.

Scrape the frozen parts around the edge back into the mixture.

Scrape the frozen parts back into the mixture until even ice crystals form.

FRUIT KEBABS WITH CARDAMOM SYRUP

Preparation time: 15 minutes + 1 hour marinating
Total cooking time: 5 minutes
Makes 8 kebabs

1/4 small pineapple, peeled
1 peach
1 banana, peeled
16 strawberries

CARDAMOM SYRUP
2 tablespoons honey
30 g (1 oz) butter, melted
1/2 teaspoon ground cardamom
1 tablespoon rum or brandy
1 tablespoon soft brown sugar

1 Cut the pineapple into bite-sized pieces. Cut the peach into 8 wedges and slice the banana. Thread all the fruit pieces onto skewers and place in a shallow dish.
2 To make the cardamom syrup, mix together the honey, butter, cardamom, rum and sugar and pour over the kebabs, brushing to coat. Cover and leave the kebabs at room temperature for 1 hour.
3 Cook the kebabs on a hot, lightly oiled barbecue flatplate for 5 minutes. Brush with the syrup during cooking. Serve drizzled with the remaining syrup, topped with ice cream.

NUTRITION PER KEBAB
Protein 1 g; Fat 2 g; Carbohydrate 16 g; Dietary Fibre 2 g; Cholesterol 6 mg; 376 kJ (90 cal)

Cut the fruit into bite-sized pieces and thread onto the skewers.

Mix together the honey, butter, cardamom, rum and sugar to make the syrup.

Cook the kebabs on a hot barbecue, brushing with the syrup during cooking.

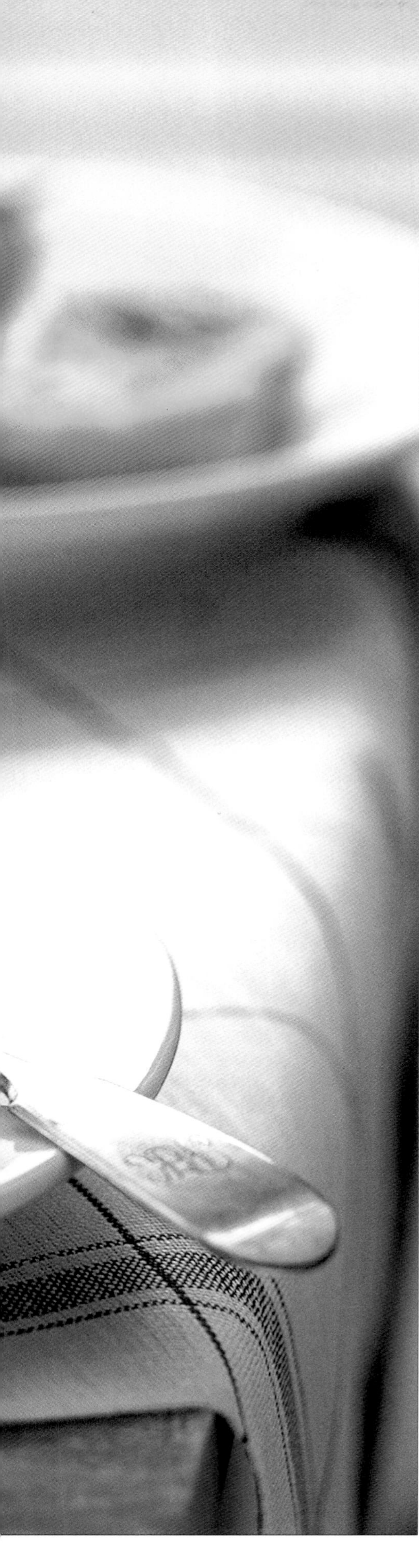

PEACHES POACHED IN WINE

Preparation time: 20 minutes
Total cooking time: 20 minutes
Serves 4

4 just-ripe yellow-fleshed slipstone peaches (see NOTE)
2 cups (500 ml/16 fl oz) sweet white wine such as Sauternes
3 tablespoons orange liqueur
1 cup (250 g/8 oz) sugar
1 cinnamon stick
1 vanilla bean, split
8 fresh mint leaves
mascarpone or crème fraîche, to serve

1 Cut a small cross in the base of each peach. Immerse the peaches in boiling water for 30 seconds, then drain and cool slightly. Peel off the skin, cut in half and carefully remove the stones.
2 Place the wine, liqueur, sugar, cinnamon stick and vanilla bean in a deep-sided frying pan large enough to hold the peach halves in a single layer. Heat the mixture, stirring, until the sugar dissolves. Bring to the boil, then reduce the heat and simmer for 5 minutes. Add the peaches to the pan and simmer for 4 minutes, turning them over halfway through. Remove with a slotted spoon and leave to cool. Continue to simmer the syrup for 6–8 minutes, or until thick. Strain and set aside.
3 Arrange the peaches on a serving platter, cut-side-up. Spoon the syrup over the top and garnish each half with a mint leaf. Serve the peaches warm or chilled, with a dollop of mascarpone or crème fraîche.

NUTRITION PER SERVE
Protein 3 g; Fat 6.5 g; Carbohydrate 74 g; Dietary Fibre 2 g; Cholesterol 19 mg; 1900 kJ (455 cal)

NOTE: There are two types of peach, the slipstone and the clingstone. As the names imply, clingstone indicates that the flesh will cling to the stone whereas the stones in slipstone or freestone peaches are easily removed without breaking up the flesh. Each has a variety with either yellow or white flesh, and all these peaches are equally delicious.

Peel the skin away from the cross cut in the base of the peaches.

Simmer the wine, liqueur, sugar, cinnamon and vanilla bean.

PLUM COBBLER

Preparation time: 25 minutes
Total cooking time: 40 minutes
Serves 6

750 g (1 1/2 lb) plums
1/3 cup (90 g/3 oz) sugar
1 teaspoon vanilla essence

TOPPING
1 cup (125 g/4 oz) self-raising flour
60 g (2 oz) unsalted butter, chilled and cubed
1/4 cup (60 g/2 oz) soft brown sugar
1/4 cup (60 ml/2 fl oz) milk
1 tablespoon caster sugar

1 Preheat the oven to 200°C (400°F/ Gas 6). Cut the plums into quarters and remove the stones. Put the plums, sugar and 2 tablespoons water in a pan and bring to the boil, stirring, until the sugar dissolves.
2 Reduce the heat, then cover and simmer for 5 minutes, or until the plums are tender. Remove the skins if you prefer. Add the vanilla essence and spoon the mixture into a 3 cup (750 ml/24 fl oz) ovenproof dish.
3 To make the topping, sift the flour into a large bowl and add the butter. Rub in the butter with your fingertips until the mixture resembles fine breadcrumbs. Stir in the brown sugar and 2 tablespoons milk.
4 Stir with a knife to form a soft dough, adding more milk if necessary. Turn out onto a lightly floured surface and gather together to form a smooth dough. Roll out until 1 cm (1/2 inch) thick and cut into rounds with a 4 cm (1 1/2 inch) cutter.
5 Overlap the rounds around the side of the dish over the filling. Lightly brush with milk and sprinkle with sugar. Bake on a tray for 30 minutes, or until the topping is golden and cooked through.

NUTRITION PER SERVE
Protein 3 g; Fat 9 g; Carbohydrate 50 g; Dietary Fibre 3.5 g; Cholesterol 25 mg; 1245 kJ (295 cal)

Sift the flour into a bowl, then rub in the butter with your fingertips.

Stir with a flat-bladed knife, using a cutting action, to form a soft dough.

Roll out the dough to a thickness of 1 cm, then cut into rounds.

RED FRUIT SALAD WITH BERRIES

Preparation time: 5 minutes + 30 minutes cooling + 1 hour 30 minutes refrigeration
Total cooking time: 5 minutes
Serves 6

SYRUP
1/4 cup (60 g/2 oz) caster sugar
1/2 cup (125 ml/4 fl oz) dry red wine
1 star anise
1 teaspoon finely chopped lemon rind

250 g (8 oz) strawberries, hulled and halved
150 g (5 oz) blueberries
150 g (5 oz) raspberries, mulberries or other red berries
250 g (8 oz) cherries
5 small red plums (about 250 g (8 oz)), stones removed and quartered
low-fat yoghurt, to serve

1 To make the syrup, place the sugar, wine, star anise, lemon rind and 1/2 cup (125 ml/4 fl oz) water in a small saucepan. Bring to the boil over medium heat, stirring to dissolve the sugar. Boil the syrup for 3 minutes, then set aside to cool for 30 minutes. When cool, strain the syrup.
2 Mix the fruit together in a large bowl and pour on the red wine syrup. Mix well to coat the fruit in the syrup and refrigerate for 1 hour 30 minutes. Serve the fruit dressed with a little syrup and the yoghurt.

NUTRITION PER SERVE
Fat 0 g; Protein 2 g; Carbohydrate 24 g; Dietary Fibre 5 g; Cholesterol 0 mg; 500 kJ (120 Cal)

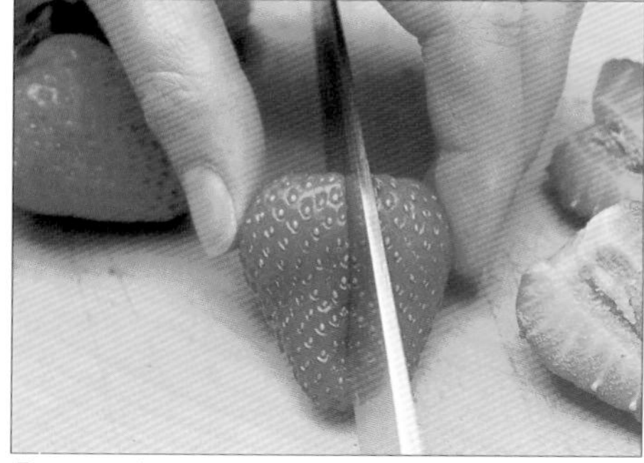

Remove the stems to hull, then cut the strawberries in half.

Boil the sugar, wine, star anise, lemon rind and water for 3 minutes.

Mix together the strawberries, blueberries, raspberries, cherries and plums.

MANDARIN ICE

Preparation time: 10 minutes + freezing
Total cooking time: 10 minutes
Serves 4–6

10 mandarins
1/2 cup (125 g/4 oz) caster sugar

1 Squeeze the mandarins to make 2 cups (500 ml/16 fl oz) juice.
2 Place the sugar and 1 cup (250 ml/8 fl oz) water in a small saucepan. Stir over low heat until the sugar has dissolved, then simmer for 5 minutes. Remove from the heat and leave to cool slightly.
3 Stir the mandarin juice into the sugar syrup, then pour into a shallow metal tray. Freeze for 2 hours, or until frozen. Transfer to a food processor and blend until slushy. Return to the freezer and repeat the process three more times.

NUTRITION PER SERVE (6)
Fat 0 g; Protein 0.5 g; Carbohydrate 5 g; Dietary Fibre 0 g; Cholesterol 0 mg; 105 kJ (25 Cal)

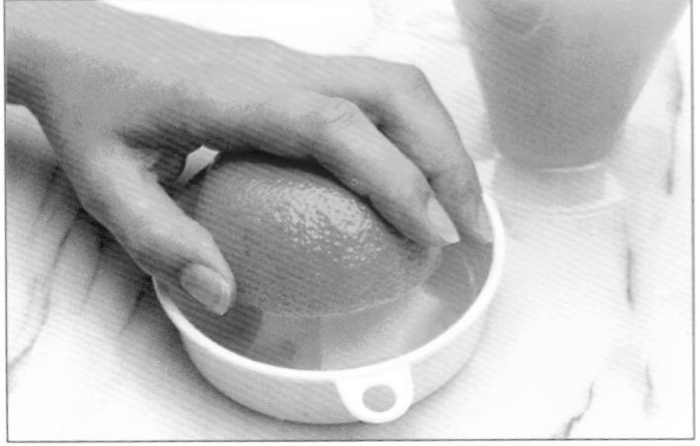

Squeeze the mandarins (as you would other citrus fruits) to give 2 cups of juice.

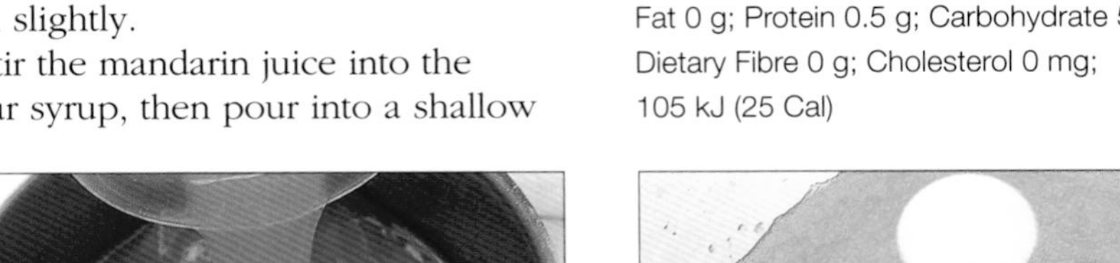

Stir the mandarin juice into the saucepan of sugar water.

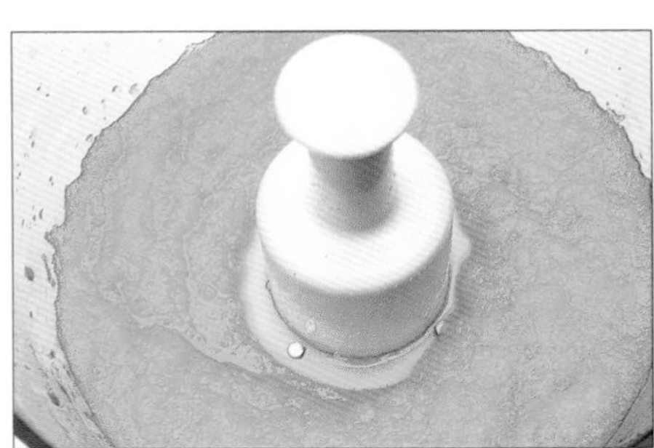

Blend the frozen mixture in a food processor until it is slushy.

APPLE SAGO PUDDING

Preparation time: 15 minutes
Total cooking time: 50 minutes
Serves 4

1/3 cup (90 g/3 oz) caster sugar
1/2 cup (100 g/3 1/2 oz) sago
600 ml (20 fl oz) fat-reduced milk
1/3 cup (55 g/2 oz) sultanas
1 teaspoon vanilla essence
pinch ground nutmeg
1/4 teaspoon ground cinnamon
2 eggs, lightly beaten
3 small ripe apples (about 250 g/8 oz), peeled, cored and very thinly sliced
1 tablespoon soft brown sugar

1 Preheat the oven to moderate 180°C (350°F/Gas 4). Grease a 1.5 litre ceramic soufflé dish. Place the sugar, sago, milk, sultanas and 1/4 teaspoon salt in a saucepan and heat, stirring often. Bring to the boil, then reduce the heat and simmer for 5 minutes.

2 Stir in the vanilla essence, nutmeg, cinnamon, egg and the apple slices, then pour into the prepared dish. Sprinkle with the brown sugar and bake for 45 minutes, or until set and golden brown.

NUTRITION PER SERVE
Protein 9.5 g; Fat 5 g; Carbohydrate 70 g; Dietary Fibre 2 g; Cholesterol 101 mg; 1495 kJ (355 Cal)

NOTE: If you prefer, you can use skim milk instead of fat-reduced milk.

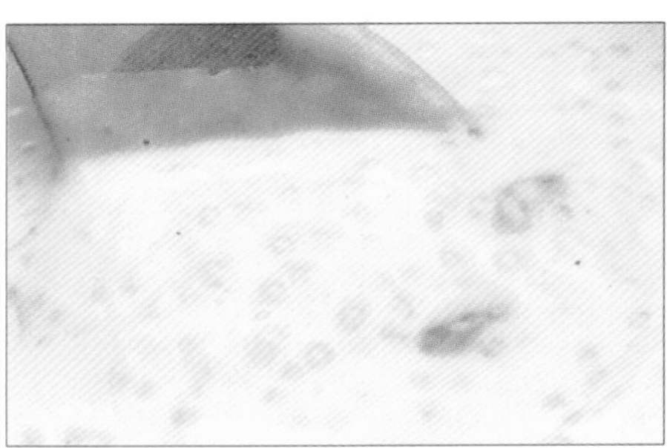

Bring the sugar, sago, milk, sultanas and salt to the boil, stirring frequently.

Stir the vanilla, ground spices, egg and apple slices into the milk mixture.

Sprinkle the surface of the pudding with the brown sugar.

Glossary

Arborio rice is a special short-grain rice used for making risotto.

Balsamic vinegar is a rich, sweet and fragrant vinegar originating from Modena in Italy. Often used in dressings.

Bok choy (Chinese chard, Chinese white cabbage, pak choi) is a popular Asian green vegetable. The smaller type is called baby bok choy or Shanghai bok choy.

Broad beans (fava beans)

Butternut pumpkin (squash)

Calamari (squid)

Cannellini beans (white beans, Italian white beans) are available canned or dried.

Capsicum (pepper)

Caster sugar (superfine sugar) is a fine white sugar with very small crystals.

Coconut cream and milk are extracted from the flesh of fresh coconuts. The cream is thick and almost spreadable. The milk is extracted after the cream has been pressed and it is thinner.

Coriander (cilantro, Chinese parsley). All parts of this aromatic plant—seeds, leaves, stem and root—can be eaten.

Cornflour (cornstarch) is a fine white powder that is usually used as a thickening agent.

Eggplants (aubergines) come in a variety of shapes, sizes and colours. Slender eggplants are also called baby, finger or Japanese eggplants, while the most commonly used are larger and rounder.

English spinach (spinach) is sometimes confused with Swiss chard but is much more tender and delicate. It requires little to no cooking but should be washed several times to remove dirt.

Feta cheese is a fresh goat's or ewe's milk cheese with a sharp, salty taste.

Fish sauce is a brown, salty sauce with a characteristic 'fishy' smell. It is made from small fish that have been fermented in the sun. It is a popular seasoning in Southeast Asian cuisine. Use it sparingly as it has a strong flavour.

Flat-leaf parsley (Italian parsley, Continental parsley)

French shallots are members of the onion family but have a sweeter flavour.

Green beans (French beans, string beans)

Icing sugar (confectioners' sugar, powdered sugar). Made by grinding granulated sugar to a fine powder.

Kecap manis is a thick, sweet soy sauce. If unavailable, use regular soy sauce sweetened with a little soft brown sugar.

Lemon grass is a thick-stemmed herb with pale leaves. It has a lemony flavour and aroma. Lemon grass can wither be used as a seasoning in stocks or soups or can be incorporated into food.

Mascarpone cheese is a soft fresh cheese made with cream to which citric or tartaric acid has been added.

Mince (ground meat)

Mirin is a sweetened rice wine and is available from Asian food stores and some supermarkets. If you can't find it, you can use sweet sherry instead.

Olive oil comes in different varieties suitable for different purposes. Extra virgin or virgin olive oil are most commonly used in dressings. Regular olive oils are preferred for cooking because of their neutral flavour. Light olive oil refers to the low content of extra virgin olive oil rather than lightness of calories.

Parmesan cheese is a hard cow's milk cheese. Sold either grated or in blocks, freshly grated has a much better flavour.

Plain flour (all-purpose flour)

Polenta (cornmeal) is ground dried corn kernels.

Prawns (shrimp) are crustaceans which come in various sizes and colours. They become opaque and turn pink once cooked.

Prosciutto is an Italian ham that has been cured by salting then drying in the air. It does not require cooking.

Rice vinegar is a clear, pale yellow, mild and sweet-tasting vinegar made from fermented rice.

Rocket (arugula, rugula, roquette) is a leaf with a peppery flavour. Often used in salads.

Self-raising flour (self-rising flour) is plain (all-purpose) flour with baking powder added.

Semi-dried tomatoes (sun-blushed tomatoes) are widely available in oil.

Snow peas (mangetout) are a variety of garden pea, eaten whole after being topped and tailed.

Spring onion (scallion, shallot). These immature onions have a mild, delicate flavour, and both the green tops and the white bulbs can be eaten raw or cooked.

Tomato paste (tomato purée, double concentrate)

Vanilla essence (vanilla extract) is made by steeping vanilla beans in alcohol and water. Look for products marked natural vanilla or pure vanilla extract and avoid the synthetic vanilla flavouring, which is made from the chemical artificial vanillan.

Wasabi paste has a pungent taste similar to horseradish.

Zucchini (courgette)

Index

Published by Murdoch Books®, a division of Murdoch Magazines Pty Ltd.

Murdoch Books® Australia
GPO Box 1203
Sydney NSW 2001
Phone: + 61 (0) 2 4352 7000
Fax: + 61 (0) 2 4352 7026

Murdoch Books UK Limited
Ferry House
51-57 Lacy Road
Putney, London SW15 1PR
Phone: + 44 (0) 20 8355 1480
Fax: + 44 (0) 20 8355 1499

Editorial Director: Diana Hill
Project Manager: Zoë Harpham
Editor: Gordana Trifunovic
Creative Director: Marylouise Brammer
Designer: Michelle Cutler
Production: Fiona Byrne
Recipes developed by the Murdoch Books Test Kitchen.

Chief Executive: Juliet Rogers
Publisher: Kay Scarlett

The Publisher gratefully acknowledges the contribution of the recipe writers, chefs, photographers and stylists who worked on the material appearing in this publication.

National Library of Australia Cataloguing-in-Publication Data
Everyday low fat. Includes index. ISBN 1 74045 234 8.
1. Low fat diet — Recipes. (Series: Everyday series (Sydney, NSW)).
641.5638

PRINTED IN CHINA by Toppan Printing Co. (HK) Ltd.
Printed 2003.

IMPORTANT: Those who might be at risk from the effects of salmonella food poisoning (the elderly, pregnant women, young children and those suffering from immune deficiency diseases) should consult their GP with any concerns about eating raw eggs.